Journal of a voyage to Australia 1855–56 by Myles Athy, a Recruit for St Mary's Monastery, Sydney

A Transcription

Anne Wark

www.ingramcontent.com/pod-product-compliance
Ingram Content Group UK Ltd.
Pitfield, Milton Keynes, MK11 3LW, UK
UKHW020615180726
13836UKWH00010B/2491

Journal of a voyage to Australia 1855–56 by Myles Athy, a Recruit for St Mary's Monastery, Sydney

A Transcription

Anne Wark

Adelaide

Photo on front cover is by Giovanni Portelli
Photo on back cover is by Anne Wark

Published by:

An imprint of the ATF Press Publishing
Group owned by ATF (Australia) Ltd.
PO Box 504
Hindmarsh, SA 5007
ABN 90 116 359 963
www.atfpress.com
Making a lasting impact

Contents

Acknowledgments vii

Introduction ix

A Biography of Myles Edmund Athy 1

- Irish Origins 3
- Downside and Polding 7
- The Voyage. The Companions 17
- Ten Years of Benedictine Life 29
- Athy's Later Years 43

The journal transcribed 59

Sources 155

Appendix 1 159

1 1855

Saturday

October 27 - The Archbishop came on board at about 6-0 A.M. Weighed Anchor at about 7-0. Were towed down the Mersey by the Tug steamboat Dreadnought which parted from us at 11-20 A.M. as the wind was fair. Fresh breeze blowing Weather ... Wind at about 11-40. Mr Livingstone, one of the owners, I believe, who came out with us from Liverpool – An agent, an extra carpenter, and a nondescript all of them were with us parted from us and returned to Liverpool by Tug steamer Dreadnought – (they gave three cheers on their departure.) Ship's Library – Breakfast 9-0. Lunch 1-30 – Heave the log – sailing before wind 10 miles per hour – The table not so full today – owing to the rolling of the ship which had an uncomfortable effect on some of our mess-mates – 4 Dinner – The table today was very thinly attended as the rolling of the ship had taken effect on the health of some of our mates – As yet I am pretty well able to eat my dinner and smoke my pipe – 5 Abreast of Holyhead – Here sad thoughts came to my mind of those dear ones I have left behind and whom I hardly dare hope to see again in this world – We have had some years of happiness together – and now our lot is to be separated and our

Acknowledgements

The task of transcribing this Journal was undertaken in order to make the original handwritten document more accessible to anyone for whom it may be of interest. After obtaining a scanned copy of the Journal in 2009 during the course of researching for my previous book, *Armour of Light*, it was apparent that a typed document would be preferable.

This outcome is the result of the generosity of many people in sharing their knowledge and skills. A debt of thanks is owed to Father Colin Fowler OP, former Parish Priest of St James' Glebe, a parish until recently referred to as being at Forest Lodge. His encouragement, knowledge, insights and suggestions have contributed enormously to this work. Brother Terry Kavenagh OSB shared a great deal of information and source material on Athy's life. Mary Jane and Michael Hogan's experience and expertise resulted in many corrections and added polish to the document. The finished product is far better for their time and efforts. The suggestions of Father Denis Minns OP on layout and his forensic attention to detail helped unravel some of the more indecipherable passages of handwriting. I also thank my husband Harry Wark and my daughter Mary for their suggestions and support during the course of the project.

I also acknowledge the permission from the National Library of Ireland, where the original Journal is held, to publish this work. Without their agreement, the task could not have been carried out.

Anne Wark
2017

happy family circle broken up - May the Will of
the Most High be done is my continual aspiration
when my heart is sad - Our dear Archbishop has
not appeared since morning — Supper 8H. Sick list
increased - The weather has cleared up. A bright moonlight
night, but unfortunately the breeze towards 11H has
fallen so that we are not making much way at
least not so much as we could wish — M.A.
Sunday Oct 28 - Very fine weather breeze very light. Bkfst at 9H
Prayers read to day by Dr Gregory, - Acts. Psalm Litany B.V. M.
Manner of hearing Mass. Gold. Man - ~~There is~~ Mass was not
celebrated to-day = The Archbishop still continues sea sick
Some of our messmates who were sick yesterday made
their appearance to-day looking particularly seedy -
some at Breakfast & others at Noon —
The time was taken to day = At abt Noon were
abreast of some rocks off the ~~wh~~ Welsh coast called
the "Bishop & his Clerks" — We shall not see
the coast of Ireland, as we have kept along the
Welsh coast to take advantage of the wind

Introduction

The opportunity to read the journal of a contemporary reveals a view of the world, a world of which both writer and reader have knowledge and experience, but perhaps differing interpretations of events. The milieu of current events will likely be known to both.

The opportunity to read a journal written 160 years ago can reveal aspects of culture and attitudes, social expectations and habits that may otherwise lie dormant. The ebb and flow of the impacts of major events for example, a war, can appear in various subtle forms. A journal, written by a young man as he sailed from Liverpool, England in October 1855 on board the *Phoenix* to Sydney, New South Wales, is such a document. The young man was Myles Edmund Athy.

Amidst the mundane notes of a long sea voyage lie comments that give clues to Athy's views of life, his values and motivation to undertake the voyage. His writing reveals something of his relationship with his family and with his God. He names some of his fellow passengers and various people of significance to him that he had known in England. This leads to an unfurling of parts of their stories, their place both in his life and in the world. Through examining the threads of human connections a great deal is revealed of the tapestry of life and, in particular, Catholic life in Sydney and beyond. The flow-on impact of the Crimean war, under way at the time of his voyage, and evidence of the effects of a ground-swell of change in the Anglican Church in England originating some decades previously emerge in their own way. The lives of some of the people Athy knew well and referred to in his writing were irrevocably changed by the forces of the Oxford Movement that arose in England some twenty-five years earlier.

I came upon evidence of the journal while preparing material for the book *Armour of Light.*[1]

Armour of Light explores various aspects of the stained glass windows in St James' Church, Forest Lodge, the parish church of an area now generally referred to as Glebe, an inner-city suburb of Sydney. The parish church was consecrated and opened in September 1878. Along the north and south walls of the church there are eighteen stained glass windows. In the western wall there is a Rose Window and a Baptistry window, and in the eastern facade behind the sanctuary there are three sets of triple lancet windows. Each window, or set in the case of the sanctuary windows, is dedicated to one or more people who had a connection with the parish. One aim of *Armour of Light* was to write some biographical notes about each person named in a window and so learn more about the social fabric of the Catholic community in Glebe in those early years.

A window on the northern wall depicting St Benedict of Nursia is dedicated to Myles Edmund Athy. It is inscribed thus:

> BLESSED ARE THE PURE OF HEART FOR THEY SHALL SEE GOD. ERECTED IN THE MEMORY OF THE REVD MYLES EDMUND ATHY OSB BY HIS BROTHER IN RELIGION REV HIGH BERNARD CALLACHOR OSB BA

Father Myles Edmund Athy OSB (1818–1891) was a Benedictine priest who served at St James' as an assistant to the Parish Priest, Father Hugh Bernard Callachor OSB (1840–1898) in the 1880s.

As the result of an internet search during the preparation of material for *Armour of Light*, I learnt that the National Library of Ireland held the Journal *Rev Myles Edmund Athy: Diary of a Voyage to Australia 1855-56.*[2] In response to my request, that Dublin institution sent me a copy of the manuscript.

The journal proved an interesting document. Athy wrote of his involvement in the routine of daily life on the vessel. He was assiduous in recording the menu for almost every meal despite the range on offer being quite repetitive. Some of his shipboard companions were

1. Anne Wark, *Armour of Light: The Stained Glass Windows of St James' Church, Forest Lodge* (Sydney: St James Parish, 2010).
2. National Library of Ireland, Manuscript Section, held at Acc 5503 Call no: Ms 42,203.

a source of amusement and, at times, an irritation. There were some major figures in the Catholic life of Sydney on board the vessel.

Being at sea for eighty days did not disconnect Athy entirely from world events. At the time of his voyage, Britain was at war with Russia in the Crimea, and references to the war occur several times in the journal.

A British Engineering Project in Crimea

The Crimean War (1853–1856) was a conflict under way at the time of Athy's voyage. The war's indirect impact on Athy's world emerges in several journal entries.

Military forces from the Ottoman Empire (later Turkey), France, Britain and the Kingdom of Sardinia (later incorporated into modern-day Italy) were arrayed against the Russian military on the Crimean Peninsula, with hostilities first erupting in October 1853.

Athy mentions several times in his journal that he was reading *The War* by William Howard Russell (1820–1907). The Editor of the *The Times*, John Thadeus Delane, had sent Russell to the Crimea in February 1854 for him to submit reports for publication. Russell was the first journalist to write from the front line in a theatre of war. *The War* was a two-part work published in 1855–56.

Russell's graphic accounts of the dreadful living and fighting conditions, details of some of the engagements between the forces, and the prevalence of serious disease, mostly cholera, amongst the British soldiers had a major impact on his British readership.

Such was the disquiet in London during 1854 that the British Parliament voted on a censure motion challenging the handling of the situation by the Conservative Government, led by the 4th Earl of Aberdeen, George Hamilton-Gordon. The Government resigned as a result of this and a change of government ensued in January 1855, with a coalition, led by the 3rd Viscount Palmerston, Henry John Temple, in power.

'The reason for Russell's despatches having such an impact on the populace was not because of their speed [of transmission] but because he was the first professional journalist to be present with a military expeditionary force and also because he reported impartially and comprehensively without censorship—the first and last time this has ever happened.'[3]

Towards the end of 1854, Sevastapol was occupied by the Russians. The city came under siege (with the British forces manning the guns trained on the besieged city). The British were based in Balaklava, only a matter of eight to ten miles to the south-west but getting a regular and adequate supply of arms and other equipment to the front line was difficult. The French too were active in prosecuting the siege. The terrain of the peninsula was very steep in places and all arms and supplies had to be transported to the front by horses. The siege had reached a stalemate and the severe conditions endured by the troops, accommodated under canvas in exposed conditions during the previous harsh winter, brought with it a very high mortality rate. What roads were there were passable when the weather was fine, but with winter came heavy rain and the ground turned to mud, hampering siege operations. Now the allied forces were facing another winter and no clear path to resolution of the siege was apparent.

According to Cooke, it was the impact of the information that Russell was communicating that prompted a British engineer who was already well experienced in the construction of railways to offer to build a railway from Balaklava to the siege lines. Samuel Morton Peto (1809—1889), proposed building a railway from Balaclava to Sevastapol to make the movement of equipment and arms much more effective. The idea was put forward in late November 1854, and by December the Secretary for War, the Duke of Newcastle, was corresponding with the Commander of the British Forces in the Crimea, Lord Raglan, on the subject.

Peto, along with fellow engineers and business partners Thomas Brassey (1805—1870) and Edward Ladd Betts (1815—1872), had a great deal of experience in railway construction. Since the 1830s railways in Britain were being built at a steady rate and between them these men had the ideas, the ability and the network of contacts to execute the proposal most efficiently. They had worked on projects in their home country, Norway, Denmark, Nova Scotia and New Brunswick.

3. Brian Cooke, *The Grand Crimean Central Railway: The Story of the Railway Built by the British at Balaklava During the Crimean War of 1854–56* (Cheshire, Knutsford: Cavalier House, 1997).

Having been commenced at the end of December 1854, the survey for the proposed track was completed by Donald Campbell in mid-January 1855. Construction commenced on 8 February and all work had been completed by 27 March 1855, seven weeks after the first tracks were laid. The seven miles of track were laid with amazing commitment and efficiency.

Cooke argues that the construction of the railway expedited the delivery of heavy arms and ammunition. Over several months and a series of attacks, Sevastapol fell to the allies in September 1855. Peace was negotiated in early 1856 and hostilities formally ceased on 1 February 1856.

In his journal entry for 12 December 1855, Athy, while not mentioning the man by name, wrote "There is on board a navvy, one of the lot sent by Peto & Company to Balaclava he is now on his way to Australia. He is a huge man looks an animal".

Peto, Brassey and Betts were also involved in the construction of railways in Queensland. In 1864 the firm were the successful tenderers for a project commencing at Ipswich. They later had involvement in other contracts in that state.[4]

The war effort in Crimea was a huge drain on the resources of Britain. Civilian ships were commandeered as transport vessels to get troops to the Crimea and the wounded back to Britain. There was a high casualty rate compounded by inadequate medical services.

The support in Britain for the war in the Crimea was not universal. In his journal entry of 9 January 1856 Athy wrote, referring to an unnamed fellow passenger, an Irish priest, one of the three diocesan priests on board, who had spent some time in Rome: 'He is all on the Russian side, hoping that they may win. He picked this Irish [bias] up in Rome where he says the feeling is all Russian.'[5]

Athy's mentor from a time in Hedon, Yorkshire, some years prior to his embarking at Liverpool, Father William Parsons, was a friend of the prominent humanitarian and philanthropist, Mrs Caroline Chisholm. Mrs Chisholm had her plans for a purpose-built vessel to transport poor emigrant women to Australia frustrated when the

---

4. *Early History of the Queensland Railways*, AE Cole (Read at a meeting of the Historical Society of Queensland, Incorporated, on April 27, 1944) see <http://espace.library.uq.edu.au/view/uq:215315/s18378366_1945_3_4_284.pdf> Accessed 20 May 2016.
5. The three diocesan priests on the *Phoenix* were Keating, McGirr and Newman.

vessel named after her, the *Caroline Chisholm* was taken in mid-1854 for troop transport to support the war effort.

The three-year-long war was brought to an end at the Congress of Paris, at the end of which the Treaty of Paris was signed on 30 March 1856, two months after the arrival of the *Phoenix* in Sydney. News of the peace treaty reached Australia in June.

* * * *

Partly due to Athy's handwriting style and partly the effect of the motion of the ship, significant sections of the work were difficult, if not almost impossible to read. I was eventually persuaded that transcribing it into a typed document would make it more accessible to others. Armed with a magnifying glass I set about the task.

The journal transcription presented here has been lightly edited. Athy tended to punctuate his writing with dashes rather than commas or full stops. His journal reads as a stream of consciousness, the conventions of grammar and spelling are not necessarily observed. I have not included the dashes but instead introduced full stops or commas where I felt it necessary to make the reader's task a little easier. These punctuation changes have been kept to an absolute minimum. Some entries were not written in date order. I have at times re-ordered the work for the sake of coherence. The journal has misspellings and crossed-out words which have not been included. The handwriting is indecipherable in some places and words or phrases, whose meaning is uncertain have been indicated by a question mark.

Athy mentioned in his writings that he kept the journal with the intention of sending it back to his family once he had arrived at his destination. He found the sea journey to be very boring. Once it left Liverpool the *Phoenix* made no landfall until Melbourne, so all Athy had to look at was sea and sky with the appearance of various birds and sea life providing the only distraction.

His writing reflects frustration at the lack of material to enliven his entries and an admission of his own lack of imagination in putting his thoughts on paper. He found the discipline of writing regularly in his journal irksome and at times he misnumbered pages, skipped some, then went back and filled in the blank pages a few days later. Homesickness was another trial for him. Athy had great faith and trusted in God's will as his guiding force. The presence onboard of ordained priests meant that Mass could be celebrated when conditions permitted and that was a great comfort to him. His birthday and particularly Christmas brought feelings of isolation from his loved ones to the surface.

Athy used the word 'Paddy' in a mildly condescending manner to refer to some fellow passengers and also to certain aspects of the Irish character. He was from a more educated section of the Irish community, Irish-born and Catholic; however, due to family circumstances, his family was not necessarily of great means. People of his ilk were well educated—often in English schools, albeit English Catholic schools.

All in all it must have been a reasonably happy trip as the passengers noted their appreciation of the Captain's efforts with a formal letter, published as an advertisement in the Sydney newspaper, the *Empire* on 31 January 1856, p 4:

[ADVERTISEMENT.]

Ship Phœnix, January, 1856.

SIR—We congratulate you most heartily on the termination of a pleasant and prosperous voyage. After our acknowledgments to the good providence of God, we hasten to assure you of the general conviction that prevails amongst us, that to your care and thorough seamanship we owe the rapidity and safety of our journey. Not one of us remembers to have ever sailed with a captain whose time and care have been more assiduously devoted to the important duties of navigation. Night and day at your post, you have inspired us with that confidence in your management and watchfulness, which is so essential to the happiness of passengers at sea. We have much pleasure in acknowledging the polite readiness of yourself and officers in attending to the wants and comforts of every one; in this respect, and in the general good order and discipline of the ship, there was nothing more that we could have desired. We bid you very gratefully good-bye, and feel we can wish you no greater success in your profession than that in every future voyage your passengers may part from you with as great a sense as we have ourselves of the kindly disposition and watchfulness of their captain.

To Captain William Moppett,
Ship Phœnix.

✠ J. B. Polding, Archbishop of Sydney	Myles Athy
H. G. Gregory, Abbot O.S.B., Vicar-General	Mary Ann Adamson
Jerome Keating, C.C.	Emily M'Carthy, O.S.B.
M. A. Cornish, O.S.B.	Caroline Amherst, O.S.B.
John M'Girr, C.C.	Eugénie Chivot, O.S.B.
Patrick Newman, C.C.	Mary Ann Unsworth
J. H. B. Curtis, O.S.B.	Catherine Dwyer
Joseph P. O'Dee	Thomas S. Makinson
	R. T. Hopkins
	J. M. Murphy

Signed—Thomas Wilde, on behalf of second cabin, intermediate, and steerage passengers.

Athy's visit to the barber is not the last activity reported in the manuscript. Turning the page on the entry recounting events of 17 January, one comes upon on entry for 2 November, 1856. By now our scribe has settled into life at St Mary's Monastery in Sydney and here he describes a boat trip, an activity for at least some of those at the Monastery on their monthly recreational day.

Their outing included a visit to the Marist Fathers Monastery at Tarban Creek. The Marists are members of a French religious order which made a major contribution to the introduction of Catholicism into the Pacific Ocean region. Athy, in his journal entry, wrote of the French priests they were visiting: 'They are under the French Bishop Dr Battallin [sic]' a fine Patriarchal looking man with a long beard, I saw him here once when on a visit to the Archbishop, one of whose suffragans he is.'

Interwoven with Athy's biography I have included a profile on some of the major figures to whom he referred in his journal. Archbishop Polding OSB, Abbot Henry Gregory OSB, Father William Lockhart, Father William Wellesley Parsons, Bishop Bataillon SM, Father Mellitus Corish OSB and Brother Anselm Curtis OSB. Each had a role, varying in significance, in Catholic life and history. Their stories add texture and context to Athy's world.

* * * *

How the manuscript made its way back to Ireland and its movements for over a century is unknown. I approached the Manuscript Section at the National Library of Ireland regarding the provenance of the item. It emerged that they had purchased it in 1999 from a bookseller, Matt McNulty. I was fortunate to make contact with Mr McNulty who wrote to me:

> I had a few early Australian books and I was going to Australia in 1999 and was bringing them with me hoping that the National Library of Australia might be interested in them to help pay for my visit. By coincidence I was talking to the keeper of manuscripts in the National Library [of Ireland] on the phone about another matter entirely and mentioned this and Myles Athy's name. Library people are wonderful—without a seconds [sic] hesitation he knew exactly what it was and the fact that Myles was accompanying I think the first catholic Bishop to NSW from Liverpool. Anyhow he said if you are selling the book we would like to acquire it so they

> made me an offer I was pleased to accept and I spent it on the trip to Australia. I had it from the 1970's. I acquired it as part of a library from a book collecting friend now diseased [sic]. She was a collector like me and I can say with certainty that she had no connection with the author or Athy family—in her younger days she worked in a second hand book store in London and like me had a great number of books which were her main interest in life. On her death I inherited part of her library and purchased the other parts as we met most weeks to discuss books and loaned them to each other.[6]

Athy: Our journal writer's surname is likely pronounced 'O'thigh'

An article in the Sydney newspaper *The Empire* of 14 February 1871 has a report titled 'The Billabong Child Murder'. A Mr Fleming is quoted:

'I don't think it necessary to give the name of the priest who advised me to disclose this matter; but the priest I made my confession to was Father O'Thigh (or Athy), at Cockatoo Island.'

Athy was appointed chaplain to the Cockatoo Island prison in 1861. The alleged offence had taken place in 1857.

My attention was directed to a passage in James Joyce's *Portrait of the Artist as a Young Man* (first published in 1916).[7] There is an exchange:

'you have a queer name, Dedalus, and I have a queer name too, Athy. My name is the name of a town. Why is the county of Kildare like the leg of a fellow's breeches? Because there is a thigh in it, he said. Do you see the joke? Athy is the town in the county of Kildare and a thigh is the other thigh.'

The *Phoenix*

By the dawn of the 1850s, shipbuilding was gathering momentum in the shipyards along the western coast of Quebec and New Brunswick,

---

6. Matt McNulty, email to author 18 November 2012.
7. T Kavenagh, 'Vaughan and the Monks of Sydney', in *Tjurunga*, 25 (1983): 178 and 228.

areas to become part of Canada when it was proclaimed a dominion in 1867. The need for larger, faster vessels was fed by the growth of immigration, the onset of gold rushes in California and then Australia and troop transport needs of the Crimean War.

The *Phoenix*, was a three masted, 906 ton sailing ship built by shipbuilder John Fisher in a major shipbuilding centre of the time, St John, New Brunswick. She was registered in June 1851 and the following year *Phoenix* went to Liverpool.[8] 1855 saw her acquired by the Liverpool Line, a shipping business started that same year by Patrick Magee, who had cut his business teeth as a marine store dealer.[9]

The naming of the vessel was indeed connected to fire and rising from ashes.

Esther Clark Wright wrote in her book, *Saint John Ships and their Builders*:

> The name Phoenix was the result of a misfortune which had occurred the previous year. On August 25, 1850, a destructive fire broke out in Fisher's shipyard at the foot of Charlotte Street. The sentry on the adjoining Queen's wharf notified John Fisher, who discovered that the fire was burning in the hold of the ship then building, and that loose chips and shavings had been gathered together under the after hatch. Before sufficient water could be brought, the whole ship was ablaze. Fortunately, the only other property destroyed was an old, condemned brig, lying by the wharf, but furniture being taken from the Fishers' house was stolen. The vessel had been sold to parties in Liverpool for £7.10s. per ton finished, and there was no insurance. A man had been seen running away from the after part of the vessel, shortly before the fire was noticed, and suspicion rested upon a former employee who

8. Esther Clark Wright, *Saint John Ships and Their Builders* (Canada: Wolfville, Canada, 1976), 82.
9. Wright, *Saint John Ships and Their Builders*, 9.

> had been dismissed and had been heard 'to use improper language' against his former employer.[10]

At the conclusion of the voyage which brought Athy to Sydney, the *Phoenix* left Port Jackson for Bombay on 26 February 1856 under William Moffat's control. A search of the record of ships visiting Sydney in subsequent years does not reveal a return visit.

Wright continued:

'The *Phoenix*, which arose from the ashes of the 1850 vessel, was based in Liverpool for 18 years, and then sold and went to West Hartlepool where she was broken up some time in the 70s.'

---

10. Wright, *Saint John Ships and Their Builders*, 108–109.

Other sources:

Lloyds Register of British and Foreign Shipping, 1855. Original material held at the University of Wisconsin –Madison Memorial Library. Microfiche accessed at Australian National Maritime Museum, Sydney.

Esther Clark Wright, *The Ships of St Martins, Ship Building and a List of Vessels Built at St Martins, New Brunswick, 1800–1899* (St John, Canada: Quarry Press, 1976).

Eileen Reid Marcil, *The Charley-Man: a history of wooden shipbuilding at Quebec 1763–1893*, Ontario, 1995.

better for me as I may have a chance of escaping sickness — went up to see a Cow which is sick. Saw her join Autumn & Pontine I felt so done up that I was obliged to put off concluding this days journal till. with Mr Com went down to ~~Cabin~~ Saloon played a game at whist; F. Keating & I against F. McE. Guru on Mr Makinson. The second game I had to get F Mullins to take my place, having to go and read pickwiff to the Archbishop. Chapter for Wednesday "Paradise of the Soul" — This was after tea night prayers — then went on deck smoked a cigar & pipe — Night very fine breeze rather slight — a lazy sort of a swell that makes the Ship roll — went to bed at 12 o'c. The whole of today we have been crossing the entrance of bay of Biscay

A Biography of Myles Edmund Athy

Nov

Thursday 22 Rose at 8.30. Rosary. Bkfst 9-30
Tea Curry. Broiled Ham. Cold Ham - Red Herrings
Rice. Stirabout. Tea. Bread & Butter — 10. Accounts
Fine day nice breeze temperature moderate
rolling ... Course S.W. by S.

Crossed the Line

Wednesday 21st It was hoped that we should have been able to have Mass today but we were disappointed as the ship rolled too much — It is the feast of the "Presentation" — Rose at 7.25. Weather fine a side wind rather ahead of us. Course S.W. by W. Lat.
Long.

Bkfst 9.30. Mince. Steak broiled Ham. Cold Ham Rice. Stirabout &c — Potatoes — at about 11.30 we Crossed The Line — We are now in the South Atlantic Ocean
Long. 12. Lunch — After lunch spent some time reading &c 3.15 Office Divine with His Grace and the Benedictine

Irish Origins

Myles Athy was born at Renville, County Galway, Ireland on 8 December 1818. He was the third son of Philip Lynch Athy and Bridget MacDonnell. He had two brothers, Edmund and Randal, and it seems that he had three sisters, Honora born c1815, Elizabeth born c 1819 and Catherine born c 1829. There is a headstone in the Oranmore Old Graveyard marking the burial place of 'Honora Lynch Athy, second daughter of Philip Lynch Athy, Esquire of Renville'.[11] She died in November 1818 at the age of three years. This graveyard at Oranmore is in the district where Renville is situated.

Records show that Myles' father, Philip Lynch Athy, was the resident proprietor of Renville in 1824 but by 1855 his brother, Randal Athy was the 'owner of Rinville [sic] House, parish of Oranmore'.[12]

In 1857 portions of the estate were advertised for sale in the Encumbered Estates Court. This Court was set up to deal with the situation in which some landowners found themselves as a result of the Famine in Ireland. Such estates may have been mortgaged and landowners, such as possibly the Athys, were unable to collect their rent. The result was a forced sale of their estates. An 1849 Act of Parliament created the Encumbered Estates Court and it had authority to sell such estates on the application of either the owner or a person who had a claim to all or part of their property. Once the sale

11. Memories in Stone. A Survey of the old graveyard at Oranmore. <http://issuu.com/oranmoreheritage/docs/memories_in_stone> Accessed 1 July 2014.
12. <http://landedestates.nuigalway.ie/LandedEstates/jsp/estate-show.jsp?id=829> Accessed 1 July 2014.

was completed, the court distributed the money among the creditors and clear title could then be given to the new owners.[13]

The site of Renville house is today part of Renville Park, an area open to the general public. One of the original buildings, known as Renville Castle, is thought to have been built in the sixteenth century and still stands, reportedly in good condition. The Athy family lived there until the construction of a new building, begun in 1820 and known as Renville, (some records spell it as Rinville) was completed.[14] That structure is now an ivy-covered ruin.

Myles' brother Randal played a role in public life in Galway. *Thom's Irish Almanac and Official Directory for the Year 1862* recorded Athy, Randal E Lynch, Renville, Oranmore as a magistrate, one among a list of almost two hundred names, with people noted to come from all parts of Ireland and as far afield as London. The same publication notes that he was a member of the Board of Superintendence of the County Prison.[15]

The Athy family was steeped in the history of early Galway, being one of fourteen families of significance, referred to as the 'Tribes of Galway', who helped settle the area in the late 1300s. The families were: Athy, Blake, Bodkin, Browne, D'Arcy, Deane, Font, French, Joyce, Kirwan, Lynch, Martin, Morris and Skerrett.

M D O'Sullivan's *Old Galway* gives some background to this group of people:

> Already in the thirteenth century we find many families bearing these familiar names domiciled in Connaught on lands won from the Irish, and some members of them were occupying high office in the service of the State.
>
> Thus it is clear that the 'Tribes' of Galway, were from their origin aristocratic conquistadors, landed gentry, characteristics which they never allowed anyone to forget when after they exchanged the sword for the pen and turned to commerce as a career in their counting houses at Galway.

13. <http://www.billmacafee.com/estates/encumberedestates/encumberedestates.htm> Accessed 1 July 2014.
14. <http://www.ciaranmchugh.com/?pagid=misty-morning-tree> Accessed 1 July 2014.
15. <http://www.libraryireland.com/Thom1862/Galway.php> Accessed 1 July 2014.

> A real landmark in the growth and development of Galway, and perhaps the soundest testimony of its increasing trade, was the building in 1320 of the main body of the church of St Nicholas. At this time also stone houses, though not as yet numerous, were coming to be erected by some of the leading families of the town, the Athys for example, the Lynches, and one or two others were already making their homes in substantial dwellings of the kind.[16]

Over the centuries these significant families were the backbone of business and community organisation in Galway, with various leadership positions in the community falling to them due to their education and social status.

His family history through the succeeding generations helps one to appreciate that, although born in Ireland, Athy had a different background to the majority of fellow countrymen. Thus the tendency at times to refer to the less well educated Irish 'paddies' is better understood.

16. MD O'Sullivan, *Old Galway. The History of a Norman Colony in Ireland*, Facsimile edition Galway (Cambridge: Heffer & Sons Ltd, 1942), 17.

very weak, he suffered from sea sickness – The holy [illegible] seen on Deck likewise, one of whom also suffered se[illegible] she appears very weak – In the morning there were some showers – There was a bark before us part of the day but we overtook her and gave her the go by – She appeared to be an English Vessel, she had lost top gallant yard – Tea at 7.30 – Afterwards some were p[illegible] whist others were reading, and some were on deck – went on Deck to have a quiet pipe – Dr Gregory is the life and soul of our party, he is so cheerful and full fun, he often has us in roars of laughter – It is delightful to have such a [illegible] with us & the fav[illegible] to be with him – Today ginger beer was produced for Dinner to Bartholomew, His Grace's servant, a glass of lo[illegible] he went to the head steward and got it for me – Night prayers at 8.50 – After which there is loitering about, an[d] punch for those who choose it – I am at a great los[s] for a tea-strainer I lose him and punch every d[illegible]

The horrid lid of this box, has just fallen whilst I was looking for something & scraped my nose and face I shall be a nice figure

Downside and Polding

St Gregory's College, Downside, a Benedictine School near Bath in England was where Myles Athy's brothers had been educated. Likewise, Myles spent about six years at the school in the 1830s. During this time it seems he was not particularly accomplished at his studies, especially in comparison to his older brother Edmund who died less than three years after he had left the school.[17] Young Myles was, however, 'very popular at Downside during his school career'.[18] It was during his schooling that Athy's life first intersected with that of John Bede Polding OSB, who was a teacher there. The foundation for Athy's commitment to travel to Australia many years later was laid in those years: 'he was educated at St Gregory's College, Downside (1831-1837), where, knowing Father Polding, subsequently first Archbishop of Sydney, he was drawn by his affection for his old master, to volunteer for the Australian mission.'[19]

Polding's episcopal ministry was a dominant thread in the history of Catholicism in nineteenth-century Australia, though he is not mentioned by name in Athy's journal. He is referred to for the first of many times in the opening line as 'Archbishop'.

Polding: The Archbishop who guided Athy's monastic experience

Born in 1794, in Liverpool, Polding was the first Roman Catholic Bishop in Australia and later Archbishop of Sydney. Both his parents

17. T Kavenagh, 'Vaughan and the Monks of Sydney', in *Tjurunga*, 25 (1983): 178–179.
18. *Downside Review* Volume X, Obituaries December 1891, 257, Benedictine University Library, Arizona.
19. HN Birt, *Benedictine Pioneers in Australia* (London: Herbert & Daniel, 1911), volume 2, 325.

had died by the time he was eight years old so his uncle, a Benedictine priest, was charged with his care. Thus began Polding's lifelong deep connection with that religious order. He was ordained a Benedictine priest in 1819 at Wolverhampton.

Then followed many years working at Downside, where there was a Benedictine monastery as well as the school. In 1834 Polding was appointed Vicar-Apostolic of New Holland, Van Diemen's Land and adjoining islands. Following this appointment, he arrived in Sydney in 1835, forty-seven years after the foundation of the Colony. His sense of duty towards the convicts was clear immediately after his arrival in Sydney:

> On reaching Sydney Polding had seen the need for an intensive mission to the convicts and arranged with Governor Bourke (who served between 1831 and 1837) for all Catholics among the newcomers, about one-third and mostly Irish, to be put in his charge for a few days. Ullathorne later recorded that Polding took the leading part in instructing and giving the Sacraments to them; 'it was a touching sight', he wrote, 'to see the Bishop with one of his criminals kneeling by his side in the sanctuary, and by word and action, instructing all through on how to make their confessions, or how to receive the Holy Communion'. By 1841 some seven thousand convicts had undertaken these exercises. This example of pastoral care set an enlivening tone that was never absent from Polding's episcopate, even in times of conflict with members of his flock, clerical and lay".[20]

Polding was a hard working man, renowned for his commitment to his pastoral duties, travelling across his vast vicariate, visiting far flung towns and settlements. He was a man of deep and abiding sanctity, generous and warm-hearted though not without some reserve, and a born missioner who scorned every personal hardship to bring religion to his widely scattered and underprivileged flock. His vicariate included the whole of Australia and in time he visited nearly all its major centres. In 1839 the London *Weekly Orthodox Journal of Entertaining Christian Knowledge* quoted a letter from

---

20. <http://adb.anu.edu.au/biography/polding-john-bede-2557> by Bede Nairn. Accessed 3 May 2015.

Sydney: 'His labors are incessant, his zeal unbounded, Protestants as well as Catholics revere him as a saint'.[21]

He was made Archbishop of Sydney and Metropolitan of New South Wales in 1842. His vision for the Catholic Church in Australia was that it would be based on the Benedictine model, with monasteries educating priests to minister to the people across the entire land.

This had impacts on some individual secular priests and other religious orders who had answered his call for assistance to work in education, health and pastoral duties in the southern continent. Ordained priests and professed religious arrived in Sydney committed to give their services to the mission work, and quickly discovered that Polding had a particular view on how their lives would be ordered. He wanted the priests to join his monastery and the nuns to comply with his views on how their affairs were managed.[22]

Polding was at times a controversial and divisive figure. Some consider that his dogged commitment to his ambition to create a Benedictine monastic church in Australia was a major fault line that ran through his administration.

During his forty-two years in Australia, Polding made several trips back to England and Europe, sometimes needing to attend to Church matters in Rome as well as seeking priests and nuns to work in his vast diocese. It was during the return leg of one of his trips to Europe that Athy sailed with him on the *Phoenix* from Liverpool in October 1855.

Almost a decade later, Athy accompanied Polding on another such endeavour, setting out from Sydney in November 1865 and arriving back in August 1867. Polding died in Sydney on 16 March 1877 and was buried in Petersham Cemetery. His remains were transferred to St Mary's Cathedral on 17 March 1901.

* * * *

During her son's years at Downside, Myles' mother was certainly aware of his shortcomings and had concerns for his future prospects. This and the impression that the family was of modest financial means is revealed in a letter she wrote on 17 August 1835 from Renville House to the Prior of Downside, Father Joseph Brown OSB:

---

21. <http://adb.anu.edu.au/biography/polding-john-bede-2557>
22. John Hosie, *Challenge: The Marists in Colonial Australia* (Sydney: Allen & Unwin, 1987), 35–43.

> I feel anxious too, to assure you that we are quite satisfied with Myles' improvement—taking into consideration his extreme giddiness which I do not think I have ever seen equalled at his age, now in 16th year—but we cannot change what is natural character—for my part I expect so little from him, in the way of mental improvement, that I feel agreeably surprised when he appears to know any thing, in this way I was astonished to hear him translate French, which he does very well for him! Of course I cannot judge of his Latin but really I look upon that as quite unnecessary for him and would prefer him to employ his time in acquiring English and arithmetic, with the addition of French. I was in hopes that he might take to the Church and with this view I was anxious about his Latin, but that expectation is quite at an end and I believe he is destined for a mercantile life.
>
> When the difficulty of acquiring any knowledge is so great, as with Myles, it is a great comfort to me to find his conduct so good, and tho' rash and hot in his temper, if I speak but one word to him, he is calmed—his health is good enough but I do not think his constitution strong—nor is his voracious appetite ever the accompaniment of sound health, I rather think it indicates something very wrong interiorly. I should be very thankful if you would take him once or twice a year to the best dentist in Bath. His teeth, I much fear, are decaying, we have no Dentist in this neighbourhood, or I should have had his teeth looked to.
>
> Mr. Athy writes in kind remembrances to you and must now apologise to you that Myles' account has been so long unsettled, but very shortly he will have it paid.[23]

What Athy did after he left Downside is unknown. An entry in his journal does reveal that he was in Hedon, Yorkshire, for a period of time during which he made a spiritual retreat. Athy mentions a

23. BM Athy to Fr Joseph Brown OSB, 17 August 1835, I 471, Birt Collection, Downside Abbey Archives. Underlining in the original.

Father William Parsons as being at the parish. Fr Parsons was Parish Priest at Hedon between 1842 and 1849.[24]

Father Parsons: A link to the Caroline Chisholm story

William Wellesley Cuthbert Parsons (c 1813—1857) was born in Yorkshire, probably about 1813. He studied at Ushaw College, Durham. This was a Catholic Seminary during the nineteenth century and is now a hall of residence of the University of Durham. From 1836 to 1841 Parsons studied at the Venerable English College in Rome, being ordained in his last year there.

His first posting was to Egton Bridge, North Yorkshire from 1841 to late December 1842. Parsons is known to have been suffering poor health during this time. He arrived in Hedon, a small town about seven kilometres east of Hull in Yorkshire, just prior to the start of the New Year in 1843, leaving on 18 August 1849.

There is evidence that his maintaining of the sacramental registers was less than adequate—there were only a few entries during his six year appointment there and, while it is known that confirmation was conferred in the Parish, there is nothing in the Parish Confirmation Register to show this.

From Hedon he went to St Marie's Sheffield in 1849–50 then to Mossley and Saddleworth, in the West Riding of Yorkshire, until 1854.

Parsons arrived in Melbourne on 12 July 1854, on board the *Ballarat*. It is thought that he came to Australia for health reasons; however, he did have a pastoral role on the vessel, an arrangement that had been determined before he left England—'the handful of Catholics on board was to be accompanied by an English priest, Fr William Wellesley Parsons.'[25]

Also on board the *Ballarat* was the noted philanthropist and humanitarian, Caroline Chisholm (1808—1877). Mrs Chisholm was returning to Australia from a period in England. She had been in the land of her birth for some time and one of her areas of work was organising suitable vessels for the transport of the poor emigrants making the journey to Melbourne and Sydney. The vessel on which she had hoped to sail, the *Caroline Chisholm*, had been taken for troop

24. See journal entry Friday 18 January 1856.
25. Mary Hoban, *Fifty One Pieces of Wedding Cake* (Kilmore, Vic: Lowden, 1973), 326.

transport when England became involved in the Crimean War. The *Ballarat* was a substitute vessel. Shortly after his arrival in Melbourne, Parsons took charge of the St Mary's Industrial Refuge for Migrants, an area of work close to Caroline Chisholm's heart.

Parsons was named in the following advertisement, published in *The Argus* on Wednesday 23 August 1854:

ST. FRANCIS'S Cathedral Church.—Two Charity Sermons will be preached for St. Mary's Industrial Refuge for Catholic Female Immigrants, on Sunday, 27th August; the morning sermon by the Rev. W. Parsons, at eleven o'clock; the evening sermon by the Rev. G. A. Ward, at seven o'clock. The offerings after each sermon will be for the above purpose. These female immigrants will be trained by a matron for domestic service. Donations of money or bedding will be thankfully received by the Rev. W. Parsons,

109 aug 26

Parsons was initially stationed at St Francis' Church in Lonsdale Street, Melbourne.[26]

The *Freeman's Journal* of Saturday 23 September 1854, reported that the Bishop of Adelaide, Right Rev Dr Murphy visited his brother prelate in Melbourne, Dr Goold, and celebrated Pontifical High Mass at St Francis' Church in that city. The article noted that, amongst others, 'the Rev. Messrs. Parsons and O'Farrell were also present'. Parsons accompanied the Bishop of Melbourne to Ballarat following the Eureka Stockade disturbance of December 1854.[27]

Parson's support for charitable work continued, as demonstrated by this advertisement in *The Age* newspaper published in Melbourne 23 June 1855.

BENEVOLENT ASYLUM.—A Charity Sermon in Aid of the Funds of this Institution will be preached in the Cathedral Church of St. Francis, Melbourne, by permission of his Lordship, the Right Rev. Dr. Goold, on Sunday, 24th June inst., immediately after divine service, by the Rev. W. W. Parsons, at eleven o'clock p m

J. HAYNES. Secretary. 109 sat jun 23

26. TJ Linane & Melbourne Diocesan Historical Commission, (1979) *Index to Abel to Zundolovich* page 13 in Volume 174.
27. Francis Mackle, *The Footprints of our Catholic Pioneers: The Beginnings of the Church in Victoria 1839–1859.* (Melbourne 1924), 122.

The Melbourne newspaper *The Argus*, in an article on 13 August 1855, reported the opening of the Roman Catholic Chapel of St Paul at Pentridge and Rev WW Parsons delivered a 'fervent discourse at the conclusion of mass'.

It was while he was still at St Francis' that the *Phoenix* arrived in Melbourne in January 1856 and Athy took the opportunity to visit his old friend. From the tone of Athy's comments, Parsons was quite unwell. He was sent to Geelong later that year.[28] He went to Kyneton, about eighty kilometres outside Melbourne in early 1857. A small booklet on the history of St Mary's Parish at Kyneton has a few lines about the Chisholm family:

'The Catholic community of Kyneton, and indeed the whole town, is privileged to count the famous Chisholm family among its members. The Chisholm family were parishioners of St Mary's in the late 1850s. In 1856 the two older sons of Caroline and Major Chisholm moved to Kyneton and opened a store in High Street. Major Chisholm often visited them and was a member of the Kyneton Magistrates' Bench.'[29]

Mary Hoban's book on Caroline Chisholm gives fuller details of Parsons stay with the Chisholm family:

> The Kyneton house, behind the store, was a many-roomed wooden dwelling, capacious enough to accommodate guests, and here, in early 1857, a friend came to stay for a while in an effort to regain his health—Fr Parsons, whose strength had been declining for a year or more. At Kyneton he was with some of the few personal friends he had in Australia. He soon became unable to move about, and it was Mary Kiniry's task to look after his needs in his last days. Fr Parsons died on 7 April 1857 and Kyneton felt a wave of sympathy for this kindly man who died in the prime of life, so far from his native Yorkshire. A huge crowd attended his funeral and though the cemetery was a mile and a half from the Chisholms' house, the coffin was carried there by relays of men on foot. Large rings had been fixed in the sides of the coffin, through which were passed strong bands of white linen. Holding these the four men marched slowly through the town followed by the

28. Linane, *Index to Abel to Zundolovich*.
29. Shane P Hoctor, *Joyful, Sorrowful, Glorious. A History of the St Mary's Parish, Kyneton 1852–1977* (Kyneton: St Mary's Parish, 1977), 17.

> people to what a reporter described as 'a strange romantic burial'. The townspeople erected a granite Celtic cross with a white marble inset over his grave.[30]

It seems the white marble inset was never inscribed, as the *Kyneton Guardian*, 13 August 1912 carried an item: 'After Many Years – A Nameless Headstone':

> Through some unaccountable oversight no name was ever carved thereon. Time passed and the cross became crooked, dejected, moss grown and weather beaten, but still nameless.
>
> Some little time since this story of 55 years ago became known to the Very Rev Dean Hegarty, V F., of St Mary's Kyneton, and he has paid a fitting and graceful tribute to the departed priest, and to the late Dean Geoghegan, by having the ravages of time and neglect obliterated from the cross, and on the marble slab carved the inscription:
>
> 'In your charity pray for the soul of Father William Wellesly Parson, of Yorkshire, England, who died at Kyneton, on April 7th, 1857, aged 43 years'.[31]

The grave of William Wellesley Parsons, Kyneton Cemetery.

30. Mary Hoban, *Fifty-One Pieces of Wedding Cake* (Kilmore, Vic: Lowden Publishing, 1973), 379.
31. It is noted that the inscribed spelling of Parsons' name is incorrect in a couple of respects.

The inscription reads:
Of Your Charity
PRAY FOR THE SOUL OF FATHER
WILLIAM WELLESLY PARSON
BORN AT YORKSHIRE ENGLAND
DIED AT KYNETON 7TH APRIL 1857
AGED 43 YEARS
R I P

I am indebted to Larina M Strauch of the Kyneton Historical Society - Secretary/Research/Archives and to Carol McQualter, Secretary Kyneton Cemetery Trust for their research and detective skills in finding the Kyneton Guardian newspaper article of August 1911 and locating Parsons' grave.
Larina Strauch supplied the two photographs.
With acknowledgements to:
Father William Ryan PP, St Mary and St Joseph, Baxtergate, Hedon.
Dr Martin Craven, author of *Faith in Adversity: the Story of the Early Catholic Missions in Holderness, in the East Riding of Yorkshire. 2004*
David Smallwood, Middlesbrough Diocesan Archivist, Curial Office, Middlesbrough.

November

Thursday 8th – Rose at 4 H 10 M. Prayers – Writing translation – Bkfst 9 H 30 M. Tom. Chops. Ham & Liver. Curry & Hash – Potatoes, these every day & Tea – Hot bread, ~~[struck out]~~ very black & Biscuits – On deck at 10 H 0 M. Beautiful weather very fine. Wind very light. N.E. Course S.S.W. All sails set save the Mizen main and the Bowsprit sails – Lat 26.56 Long 19° The day will be fearfully hot it is now only 11 H 0 M and I can scarcely bear it – A Vessel in the offing – 11 H. I came to my Cabin to write the exercise given by His Grace; by the bye he gave me a little cross for my cabin this morning – Rate of sailing 5 Knots per hour. 2 H 30. Very heavy shower – lasted for about 15 or 20 minutes rain fell in buckets full – 1 H 45. Went to read to His Grace as usual – Wind at 3.15 N.N.E. – 4 H 30 Dinner. Soup. Tom. Roast Mutton. Boiled Turkey – Ham – Sheeps head & Trotters. Curry. Vegetables Potatoes Turnips Carrots – Rice boiled Puddings – Plums & Sago – Dessert Raisins Figs [illegible] Nuts – 6 H Heard the Log. Rate of sailing 4½ Knots We had a very fine sunset this evening – but I have seen finer at Rossville – But as soon as the sun had set the sea assumed the most beautiful tint I ever beheld

The Voyage. The Companions

It was 27 October 1855 when Myles Athy, at the age of thirty-six, left Liverpool, England on board the *Phoenix* bound for Sydney, Australia. He was giving serious thought to join the Benedictine order and had decided to pursue studies. He was travelling under the guidance of Archbishop John Bede Polding OSB.

Athy's journal reveals that several priests, including Fathers Keating, Newman and McGirr were fellow passengers. The Vicar General at Sydney and Prior of the Benedictine community there, Dr HG Gregory OSB (1813–1877), was also in the travelling party as were two other Benedictines, Anselm Curtis, who was yet to be ordained and Mellitus Corish, who had been ordained in Ireland in 1845 and had joined the Benedictine community in Sydney in 1847.

The name of Henry Gregory OSB (1813–1877) appears frequently in Athy's journal. He was an enthusiastic participant in shipboard life, getting up games of various sorts to help pass the time and giving some exercise to his fellow travellers. His contribution to such diversions did not stop with the group of clerics with whom he was travelling. Athy twice mentions Gregory as having been involved in organising amusements for the steerage passengers. Athy had nothing but admiration for him: 'Dr. Gregory is the life and soul of our party, he is so cheerful and full of fun, he often has us in roars of laughter—It is delightful to have him with us rather for us to be with him.'[32]

32. Athy journal entry, Wednesday 7 November 1855.

Henry Gregory: A controversial figure in the early Australian Church

For twenty-five years Gregory served in Sydney as a loyal deputy to Polding in his role as Vicar General and also as Prior of the Benedictine Monastery. The history of the Catholic Church in Sydney shows that while Gregory did have great strengths, some of his flaws led to disharmony and division and ultimately to his being recalled to England in 1861. Mary Shanahan's book *Out of Time Out of Place: Henry Gregory and the Benedictine order in colonial Australia*, published in Canberra in 1970, provides a detailed study of his career and I have relied on it quite heavily.

Henry Gregory was born in 1813 at Cheltenham, Gloucestershire (England) and educated at the Benedictine schools at Douai, northern France from 1827 to 1830, followed by some years at Downside.

In 1833 he joined the Benedictine order at Downside where Polding was his novice master. Gregory arrived in Sydney with the newly appointed Bishop for the Sydney mission on the *Oriental* from Liverpool on 27 March 1835. Gregory had been ordained a sub-deacon in September the previous year, having been professed in June 1834. Polding ordained Gregory a priest in Sydney in 1837. After returning to Europe in 1840, Gregory went to Rome where he was awarded a Doctorate of Divinity by Pope Gregory XVI. He subsequently returned to Sydney.

By 1843 Polding had gained the consent of Rome to formally establish a Benedictine Monastery in Sydney. This was something that the Archbishop had been working towards. A short time after he had first arrived in the colony in 1835, a seminary had been set up at his residence at Woolloomooloo. In January 1838 it was transferred to buildings in the grounds of the cathedral and become known as St Mary's. It was there that the monastery was established in 1843 with Gregory appointed as Prior. In this role he was responsible for organising the life of the monks and training the men in his care according to the Rule of Benedict. Gregory was given a tall task indeed. He was just thirty years of age and had only lived the monastic life for two years as a novice and junior religious at Downside in 1833 and 1834, almost ten years previously.

Clearly Polding had great confidence in him. In a letter written from Sydney some years earlier, in May 1836 to his cousin, TP

Heptonstall OSB, a Downside Monk who also acted as Polding's agent in England, the Sydney Bishop was discussing the clerical situation he was dealing with. He commented that 'Mr Gregory will take charge under me of the Seminary which I am determined to commence on the 29th June. I have had many difficulties and must expect more and greater, but I trust we shall get through.'[33] At that time Gregory was yet to be ordained and was just twenty-three years of age.

In 1844 he was appointed as Vicar General, effectively Polding's 'right hand man'. Gregory was reputedly a man who went straight to the point with little thought either for the feelings of others who might be involved in a given interaction, or of the consequences of his actions. He was capable of wonderful acts of charity, but the role of a Vicar General required more than that.

His administrative methods alienated several groups of religious men and women who had arrived in the colony in response to requests for assistance with teaching, health and social work among the population. The Christian Brothers returned to Ireland and some of the Irish Sisters of Charity moved to Van Diemen's Land rather than accept Gregory's meddling in their internal affairs.

There were many aspects to the complex veins of discontent flowing through both fellow clergy and lay people in the colony that found a focus in Gregory. The issue of English Benedictine leadership of the mainly Irish secular priests and a largely Irish Catholic community was certainly part of the problem. Gregory's style of governance was also working against him.

In the early to mid 1850s, there was unrest within the walls of the Benedictine Monastery itself with a variety of matters of concern. Gregory's dual role as Prior of the monastery and Vicar General in Sydney was one of the grievances. In March 1854, Polding, accompanied by Gregory, left for Rome. Polding made it known that he intended to resign as Archbishop as he felt he had lost the confidence of his people.

In September 1854 two of the young monks close to the centre of the discontent at the Monastery, Anselm Curtis and Mellitus Corish, took themselves to Rome without the permission of their superiors.

33. Polding to TP Heptonstall, Bishop's House (Sydney) 1 May 1836. *Polding Letters*, volume 1, 59.

With Polding and Gregory away from the colony, they did not seek permission from anyone in Sydney.

Pope Pius IX did not accept Polding's resignation and after conducting other church business in Rome and England, he and Gregory prepared to return to Sydney.

Gregory, along with Polding, Athy our journalist and the two monks in question, Corish and Curtis, were in the group of clerics who boarded the *Phoenix* at Liverpool in October 1855 for the voyage south, arriving back in Sydney in January 1856. The matters that had been of concern to Corish and Curtis had reached a conclusion.

Polding remained as confident in Gregory's abilities as always. In 1859, during the necessary consultative process between Polding, Bishops Goold in Melbourne and Willson in Hobart about the establishment of new dioceses and the appointment of Bishops to head them, Polding suggested that Gregory be appointed as Bishop of Maitland, with the recommendation:

'No one on the mission has had greater experience; no one has laboured with more assiduity, has live a more disinterested life, has more eminently fitted himself for the Episcopacy by the exact fulfilment of all the duties of a zealous, pious priest; his health is rather delicate; his removal from the annoyances of insolent purse proud men in Sydney will be of service.'[34]

For a variety of reasons the appointment did not go ahead.

In 1859 Gregory caused uproar amongst Sydney's Catholic community when, feeling the man's skills warranted the position, he appointed a Protestant, Doctor Bassett, to the committee of management of the Catholic orphanage at Parramatta. From our perspective in the early 21st century, such a move would hardly raise an eyebrow, but in a society still riddled with sectarianism, the Irish laity used this as fuel to the fire of anti-Gregory sentiment. Accusations, justified or not, were freely aired against him, and in 1861 he was recalled to England.

Polding had always relied heavily on Gregory for advice and support, and he felt his absence deeply. A perusal of the Polding Letters reveals a great deal of correspondence with Gregory over the subsequent years, sounding him out on many administrative matters,

34. Polding to Goold, Sydney 11 February 1859. Reprinted in Archbishop Patrick Francis Moran, *History of the Catholic Church in Australasia* (Sydney 1894), 784.

seeking his counsel and generally sharing the heavy burden under which Polding felt that he laboured.

Gregory may have come to know Myles Athy quite well, having spent close to three months together in the confines of the *Phoenix* during the voyage to Sydney. Gregory resumed duties as Prior of the Monastery at St Mary's which Athy joined on his arrival in Sydney in 1856.

Whilst Polding was travelling with Athy in England and Europe almost a decade later in 1865-66, Athy's name appeared in several letters the Archbishop wrote to Gregory, by then living in England. In them Polding often mentioned Father Edmund, being Athy's name in religion, and shared with Gregory some amusing anecdotes and at times some frustrations that arose in that period when the Archbishop had the company of Athy as his carer and travelling companion.

The allegations that prompted Gregory's recall were eventually proven to be unjust and he was given permission to return to Sydney but chose not to, much to Polding's disappointment. He was living in Broxwood, Herefordshire and was quietly involved in the life of the local community.

Cardinal Moran relates that following Gregory's return to England:

> He in after years lived as chaplain with the family of Colonel Cox at Broxwood, and devoted himself to the missionary duties in the neighbourhood. Through his piety and zeal, a flourishing Catholic congregation was gradually formed in that hitherto exclusively Protestant district. He was respected and beloved by all for his affability and laborious self-sacrifice, and his demise, on July 19th 1877, was lamented alike by Protestants and Catholics. His remains repose in the pretty little cemetery at Broxwood.[35]

Fellow Phoenix passengers and Benedictines, Anselm Curtis and Mellitus Corish also settled back into monastic life in Sydney at the end of the *Phoenix* voyage. Their backgrounds, some of the reasons for their being in Europe prior to boarding the *Phoenix* and their subsequent years in Australia comprise a small chapter in the Catholic history of Sydney.

35. Archbishop Patrick Francis Moran, *History of the Catholic Church in Australasia*, 461.

Corish and Curtis: Companions on the journey

Anselm Curtis (1829–1909) and **Mellitus Corish** (1818–1864), were two of the party on board the *Phoenix* travelling with Polding on the voyage back to Sydney in 1855-56. The events leading to their presence on the vessel were not without controversy. Corish was not named in Athy's diary. He was, however, very much part of events leading to the two monk's going to Europe.

* * * *

John Henry Curtis was born in Sydney in 1829. His grandfather Henry Parsons was reputedly a first fleet marine. Mary Parsons, one of Henry Parsons' daughters, married James Curtis in 1828 and on 28 June 1829 their son John Henry Curtis was baptised. The Curtis family lived in Sydney and by December 1845 John had joined the Benedictine monastic community at St Marys and was given the name in religion of Anselm.

Curtis was professed early in 1848 along with an Irishman from County Wexford, an ordained priest, Michael Andrew Corish who had arrived in Sydney in 1847. He was known in religion as Mellitus.

Kevin Livingston, the author of the article 'Anselm Curtis' in *Tjurunga*, 8 (December 1974), wrote that there was a degree of unrest amongst the monastic community at St Marys from late 1849. One of the matters at the heart of the problem was the question being entertained by some of the monks regarding the validity of their monastic vows. HN Birt, in *Benedictines in Australia*, wrote that Archbishop Polding was aware of the matter by 1853 at least, and did attempt to resolve the issue, apparently unsuccessfully. Other points of contention amongst the monks related to the difficulties some perceived in having secular priests serving in what was being developed as a diocese in the colony with a decidedly Benedictine flavour. Another area of discontent was in regard to Very Rev Dr Henry Gregory OSB in his dual roles as Vicar General and Prior of the monastery.

In mid-March of 1854 Archbishop Polding stunned the Catholics of Sydney when he left unannounced, bound for Rome with, it was reported, the intention of submitting his resignation. This was due in part to his impression that he had lost the confidence of the people under his archiepiscopal charge. A public meeting which was called immediately following his departure was told that the matters that prompted this extreme response were related to the management of the Catholic Church in the colony, and some of those matters were said to be of a purely clerical nature.[36] He tendered his resignation to Pope Pius IX, but it was refused.

As it transpired, Anselm Curtis and Mellitus Corish left for Rome in September that same year without the permission of their superiors. Curtis and Corish were armed with a petition outlining the grievances which they wished to present on behalf of themselves and others of a like mind to the Sacred Congregation De *Propaganda Fide* in Rome.

As recorded by Birt in *Benedictines in Australia* there were essentially three points to their document:

- A Reclamation against their solemn Religious Profession
- A most humble petition, if their vows proved to be valid, for secularisation
- A petition for the removal from all authority over them of the Very Rev Dr Gregory, V.G. and Prior.[37]

Such a course of action attracted public attention in Sydney, not least as the result of an item which appeared on 22 September 1854 in the *Empire* and an identical item in the following day's copy of the *Freeman's Journal.*

> The following letter from these gentlemen, who left Sydney by the Steamer *Madras*, has been handed to us for publication: -
>
> 'Dear Friends—At this very instant, we have got word to hasten on board the *Madras*—for us a sudden and unwelcome message indeed—as it announces our departure from those we loved so sincerely, and shall ever hold most dear—those to whose services our lives have been, and with God's assistance, ever shall be devoted. Your generosity towards us has even surprised ourselves, who had so many previous opportunities of knowing your kindly feelings and warm hearts. We thank you—most gratefully thank you.

36. 'Departure of Archbishop Polding Public Meeting', in *Freeman's Journal*, 1 April 1854, 8–10.
37. HN Birt, *Benedictines in Australia*, Volume II p 216.

> Some rumours have reached us which demand contradiction. It has, we believe, been said that we are going to Rome in opposition to his Grace the Archbishop. No assertion could be more untrue or unjust than this. We love our dear and Venerable Archbishop most sincerely, and it is our most consoling hope to return to this lovely land in company with his Grace. Although we may not now more fully explain the object of our journey, we are sure it will satisfy our dear friends to know, that we are acting sincerely and conscientiously, and that we shall soon, with God's assistance, return to them, and give them every satisfaction they may require.
>
> Again, dear, good, generous friends—farewell!
> MA Corish
> JHA Curtis
> Sydney, September 20th 1854.'[38]

The local Superior communicated as much to Polding.[39] On hearing of the events, Polding, himself in Rome, wrote to GF Cardinal Fransoni, the Prefect of the Congregation of *Propaganda Fide* on 16 December of that year:

> It is my painful duty to inform Your Eminence that two of the Community of St Mary's in Sydney have arrived in Rome without any permission from their Superior. They are Mellitus Corish, Priest, and Anselm Curtis, Deacon. They spend their time now in pleasure in the City. This occupation hardly appears to me to be suitable to the unhappy state in which these victims of voluntary deception happen now to be. I very respectfully request Your Eminence to consider the deplorable result that such conduct of these young persons, if let go unpunished, would produce in the infant Church in Australia.[40]

38. 'The Rev Mr Corish and the Rev Mr Curtis', *Empire*, 22 September 1854, 6 and also published in *Freeman's Journal*, 23 September 1854, 10.
39. Polding to unknown bishop, S Maria in Posterula, 9 December 1854. *Polding Letters*, volume 2, 217–218.
40. Polding to Fransoni, S Maria in Posterula, 16 December 1854. *Polding Letters*, volume 2, 218–219.

Propaganda responded in the negative on all points of the petition, so their trip was in vain. Their course of action, however, required some consequences.

Polding indicated in a letter to Pope Pius IX in January 1855 that Curtis and Corish 'having mended their ways and repented of their fault... they retired to S Eusebio to make the spiritual exercises'.[41] Saint Eusebio was a small church in Rome administered by a community of Jesuits. The 'Spiritual Exercises' is a thirty day Jesuit retreat which has the reputation for being quite rigorous.

Curtis and Corish were then sent to the Benedictine Monastery at Subiaco,[42] south-east of Rome, to be under the care of the Abbot-President there, Abbot P F Casaretto OSB.

The two monks remained there several months before returning to Rome. In October 1855 they found themselves on the *Phoenix* for the return voyage to Sydney. Athy's writing in his journal reveals nothing of this background to the presence of Curtis and Corish on the vessel, if indeed he was aware of it at all. Gregory, of course, was also on the vessel. There was a very public display of affection from the people of Sydney on the return of the Archbishop in January 1856. At the conclusion of the formal welcoming ceremony in St Marys Cathedral, Corish spoke on behalf of himself and Curtis and expressed an apology for their actions which Polding then publicly accepted.[43] Another eighteen months were to pass before Curtis' ordination to the priesthood in June 1857. In the meantime, he worked as the President of St Marys Seminary which was the day school for younger boys, situated near the Cathedral. Following his ordination, he was Master of Novices at Lyndhurst in The Glebe and remained in charge of the school. The novitiate had moved from St Mary's to Lyndhurst in 1857. Lyndhurst was not without its problems at that time. Some Catholic parents considered the standard of education offered to the boys at Lyndhurst to be insufficient to equip their sons for life and chose instead to send them to Europe for their studies.[44] [45] The school was trying to be all things to all parents, offering a classical education

41. Polding to Pope Pius IX, Rome, 10 January 1855. *Polding Letters*, volume 2, 220.
42. Polding to Casaretto, Rome, 15 March 1855. *Polding Letters*, volume 2, 223.
43. 'Arrival and Reception of the Archbishop', in *Freeman's Journal* 2 February 1856, 3.
44. John Hosie, *Challenge: The Marists in Colonial Australia,* (Sydney: Allen & Unwin, 1987), 133.
45. 'Father Rocher's Departure', in *Freeman's Journal*, 20 April 1859, 2.

(Classical Greek, Latin, French, Logic along with English History and Religion were subjects offered). From 1861 it attempted to attract students who wished to engage in commercial pursuits so now it was a preparatory college for aspirants to university, a monastic novitiate and a training school for those with a commercial orientation. Through all this, Curtis was the main public figure associated with the College.

His connection ended abruptly following the conclusion of the 1863 school year when he left the Benedictine community, the priesthood and Sydney to move to Melbourne. He settled there, subsequently married, raised a family and spent the next forty-five years in the southern city.

Livingston wrote that Curtis' life was in some ways tragic. He commented that Curtis was a participant in significant events in the story of Sydney Benedictines and he embodied many of their strengths and weaknesses. Curtis impressed people with his scholarship throughout his life. Sadly, for him, he lived many years without a dispensation from his monastic vows and priesthood, in spite of his efforts to have the matter resolved. Even in 1903, at the age of 74, when he wrote to Cardinal Moran seeking his intervention, he was refused an interview.[46]

It seems he did succeed eventually, as his obituary in the *Austral Light* stated that:

'On 5th July 1909, fortified with the rites of Holy Church, Mr J H B Curtis passed into "The world beyond the grave," at the ripe age of eighty-three years. During his last illness he was visited by his Grace the Archbishop and the Very Rev. Dean Phelan.'[47]

The *Austral Light* was a monthly literary publication in Melbourne to which Curtis contributed, over many years, numerous articles on a variety of subjects. Some were reflections on his time in the monastery. For three decades he was a member of a subscription library and literary organisation, the Melbourne Athenaeum, taking the role of Secretary for twenty-eight of those years.

Livingston made an interesting point about the man: 'When he left the Benedictines in 1864 Curtis ceased to bear the religious

46. K Livingston, 'Anselm Curtis', in *Tjurunga*, 8 (Dec 1974): 215.
47. 'The Late JHB Curtis', in *Austral Light* (August 1909): 575. It is noted that the age quoted for him is incorrect.

name of 'Anselm'. For the rest of his life, however, John Henry Curtis continued to add a third Christian name to his baptismal names: viz Benedict. Thus, to the end of his days, 'J H B Curtis' wanted to be known as a son of Benedict.'[48]

* * * *

Michael Andrew Corish was born in Wexford, Ireland in 1818. Following his boyhood schooling he studied at the diocesan seminary in Wexford before continuing his studies to St Kieran's College in Kilkenny. Ordination followed in 1845. He offered himself to the missionary church in Sydney and sailed from Liverpool, England on 27 November 1846 on board the *Sea Nymph* arriving in Port Jackson on 31 March 1847.

He joined the Benedictines at their novitiate at St Marys almost immediately and took the name in religion of Mellitus. He was professed in July 1848. He then worked in Balmain, Brisbane Water and briefly at Wollongong before being appointed to St Benedict's on Parramatta Street (now Broadway) in October 1850. The population of the Sydney area was growing rapidly and with it the need for more churches. While based at St Benedict's, Corish was involved in the fund raising efforts that eventually saw the building become debt free. He was present at the consecration of the building in February 1862.

During his time at St Benedict's, Corish also undertook work that saw the erection of churches at Waterloo and Botany. The foundation stone for The Church of Our Lady of Mount Carmel at Waterloo was laid on 15 August 1859 and the completed building was blessed and opened on 7 April 1861. Corish officiated at the laying of the foundation stone for St Bernard's Church at Botany on 11 September 1860, the inclement weather having prevented Archbishop Polding from venturing out for the ceremony. Polding officiated at the blessing and opening of St Bernard's on 29 December 1861 with the Mass being celebrated by Father Corish.

It was during this almost thirteen year period when he was based at St Benedict's that he and Anselm Curtis undertook the controversial trip to Rome and subsequent return on the *Phoenix* in January 1856.

48. Livingston, 'Anselm Curtis', 207.

Corish was a man with a social conscience, reportedly being involved in the Randwick Destitute Children's Asylum, The Sydney Infirmary, the House of the Good Shepherd, St Vincent's Hospital, St Benedict's Catholic Young Men's Society and he was a Fellow of St John's College, a residential College of the University of Sydney. He was appointed to Bathurst in early 1864 and died there after a short illness on 30 June of that year at the age of forty-six. He was buried at Bathurst.[49] [50]

49. 'The Late Reverend MA Corish', in *Freeman's Journal*, 6 July 1864, 5.
50. HN Birt, op cit, Volume II p 216-222.

Ten Years of Benedictine Life

As preparation for his life as a Benedictine priest during the twelve-week voyage, Athy was tutored almost daily by Archbishop Polding in studies of a spiritual nature, and in Latin. Following his arrival in Sydney on 26 January 1856, Athy joined the Benedictine religious community at St Mary's Priory, which was attached to St Mary's Cathedral at that time. He took the name 'Edmund', thus becoming known in religion as Brother Edmund. With the arrangement of the various official positions within that community, we read in the Benedictine Journal entry of 26 May that year:

> Br Anselm (Curtis) receives the office of the Dean of the Monastery, the office of infirmarian in which office he is to have one of the choir postulants, Br Edmund (Athy) as assistant, the office of the 1st Cantor, and that of the Master of the Choir.

The Journal entry continues:

> It will be seen from the foregoing distribution that all the offices in the house have been provided for. It may also have been remarked that two of the postulants have been appointed as assistants in certain offices, to others holding office. They are, in fact, appointed to the offices in which they are assistants, but owing to their not being Religious, they could not, in a direct manner, be appointed to the office; so an indirect means was had recourse to. Of course, they would not have received the appointments by any means, were there Religious in the house to supply their place. [51]

51. *Benedictine Journal* entry 26 May 1856, Sydney Archdiocesan Archives.

Archbishop Polding was closely involved in the education of his future priests. At the end of his first year at the Seminary, Athy, along with fellow postulant Brother John Dwyer, examined in Theology 'during two hours'.[52] Athy was given tonsure and minor orders by Archbishop Polding on the Feast of Saints Peter and Paul, 29 June 1857, at St Mary's Cathedral.[53] On the same occasion, the first Sydney born priest, Anselm Curtis OSB, was ordained. Athy was ordained a priest by Archbishop Polding at St Mary's Cathedral on 22 December 1860.[54] As a newly ordained priest, Athy spent the next few years based in Sydney. In January 1861 he was appointed to officiate at Cockatoo Island which housed a convict prison in Sydney Harbour. The island is just off the suburb of Balmain and comprised part of the Balmain Mission.[55]

In the next year or two, the *Freeman's Journal*, a Catholic newspaper which was first published in Sydney in 1850, carried reports that mention Athy's presence at various ceremonies in other parts of Sydney to mark 'Forty Hours Devotions',[56] the profession of nuns in the order of Sisters of the Good Shepherd[57] and involvement in Christmas services at the Cathedral.[58] March 1862 found him at the consecration of St Benedict's Church on Parramatta Road.[59]

In June 1862, Father Athy accompanied Archbishop Polding on a visitation tour of the southern districts of New South Wales, attending to the pastoral and sacramental needs of the people in isolated communities, taking in Goulburn, Yass and Albury. They also intended to visit the Lambing Flat and Lachlan Diggings,[60] but the latter two destinations were not accessible due to the condition of the roads.[61] The trip took about three months. On 27 July the party was at St Bede's, Braidwood, to administer the sacrament of Confirmation.[62]

52. *Benedictine Journal,* 8 October 1856.
53. 'Saints Peter and Paul', in *Freeman's Journal,* 4 July 1857, 2.
54. See *Freeman's Journal,* 26 December 1860, 2. No title.
55. 'Ecclesiastical Preferments' in *Freeman's Journal,* 5 January 1861, 2.
56. 'Quarant'ore', in *Freeman's Journal,* 19 June 1861, 7.
57. 'Profession at the Good Shepherd', *Freeman's Journal* 10 July 1861, p 4.
58. 'Saint Mary's Cathedral-Christmas Services', *Freeman's Journal* 28 December 1861, p 6.
59. 'Consecration of St Benedict's', in *Freeman's Journal,* 22 March 1862, p 5-6.
60. 'Lane Cove', in *Freeman's Journal,* 21 June 1862, 5.
61. 'St Leonards', in *Freeman's Journal,* 19 July 1862, 7.
62. 'Braidwood', in *Freeman's Journal,* 30 July 1862, 2–3.

They also visited Araluen, Reidsdale, Tumut, Gundagai, Jugiong, Binalong, Queanbeyan, Bungendore, Boro and Berrima, celebrating Mass and administering Confirmation.

In September 1862, Father Athy was appointed 'for the mission of Orange'.[63] While in Orange his concern for seeing justice done for others is revealed in a newspaper article. The *Freeman's Journal* of Wednesday 28 January 1863, described a public meeting in that town addressed by Athy. He spoke eloquently of the strong feelings of indignation felt by many in the local community following the verdict of justifiable homicide in the trial of a police officer, at whose hand one Cornelius Boyd had died. The meeting had hoped to persuade the Attorney General to institute a new and, in their view, fairer trial.[64] Their endeavours proved fruitless.[65]

Archbishop Polding made another of his pastoral visits to the country in late 1863 and in the *Freeman's Journal* of 2 December that year, it is stated that Father Athy was with him when he celebrated Mass at Burrowa, Walla, and administered the sacraments of Confirmation and First Communion at Grabben Gullen.[66] Burrowa (now spelt Boorowa) and Grabben Gullen are in the vicinity of Goulburn, being about fifty-five kilometres apart. It is worth remembering that Archbishop Polding was around sixty-nine years of age by this time, demonstrating commitment and stamina in carrying out his pastoral duties.

The clerical changes recorded in the *Freeman's Journal* of 12 March 1864, state that Athy was to return to Sydney.[67] The same publication, in its edition of 2 April 1864 reports on a farewell to Father Athy by the people of Orange, and notes the great affection and high esteem in which he was held by them. Athy's comments mention that in coming back to Sydney: 'He himself would be a gainer, for it would enable him to obtain the society of other clergymen, which he felt he much wanted. Previous to coming here he had been used to such companionship and he now felt a hiatus in its absence.'[68]

63. 'Religious Memoranda', in *The Sydney Morning Herald*, 20 September 1862, 7.
64. 'The Death of Cornelius Boyd – Public Meetings', in *Freeman's Journal*, 28 January 1863, 5.
65. 'The Late Connell Boyle', in *Freeman's Journal*, 4 March 1863, 5.
66. 'Country Districts', in *Freeman's Journal*, 2 December 1863, 3.
67. 'Clerical Changes', in *Freeman's Journal*, 12 March 1864, 5.
68. 'Presentation of a Farewell Address to the Rev Father Athy, Orange', in *Freeman's Journal* 2 April 1864, 2–3.

Archbishop Polding considered Athy to have great skills as a missionary as in a letter he wrote to Abbot H G Gregory OSB, Athy was briefly mentioned as being 'a first rate Miss(ionary)'.[69] It had been four years since Gregory was recalled to England after twenty-five years service in New South Wales. As mentioned earlier, Gregory was to remain a lifelong friend and confidant to the Archbishop.

Father Athy, along with Father Bede Sumner, accompanied Dr Polding, on what, for the Archbishop, was to be his last visit to the Holy See. They set out from Sydney on the vessel *Bombay* on 22 November 1865. The intention of the trip was, among other things, to attempt to garner more volunteers for the apostolate in Australia.

It seems that Father Athy accompanied Polding to be his companion and carer.

> Fr Edm. takes the best of care of me and so be quite easy on that account.[70]

Other letters which Polding wrote during that trip give a glimpse of aspects of Fr Athy's personality.

> F Edm is writing no end of letters descriptive of things living and inanimate. His hat is considered meditatively. I am sure he will write about [it]—he esteems [it] such a curiosity in its way. It will be deposited in the Museum of Lyndhurst on his return.[71]

They visited Monte Cassino (in Italy), and then on to Rome. In the course of travelling from there to London, they were to pass through Turin. On arrival in that city, however, the Archbishop and Father Athy experienced an unexpected turn of events.

> My Journey from Rome had its monotony broken by a little incident. I and F. Edm. were arrested at Turin, detained and taken to the Police Office, examined very closely and then

---

69. Polding to Gregory, Sydney, 21 September 1864. *Polding Letters*, volume 3, 167.
70. Polding to M Scholastica Gibbons, no address, but apparently after the voyage had started, 2 December 1865. *Polding Letters*, volume 3, 198.
71. Polding to Sr Justine Merewether, English College, 22 February 1866. *Polding Letters*, volume 3, 204–205.

> liberated. In vain we pleaded that we were British subjects and as such entitled to travel through Italy without passports. To no purpose we showed the passport received from Gov. Of Malta. About midnight we were allowed to return to an hotel. I wrote at once to the Ambassador at Florence, Mr Eliot, and took the precaution of sending a copy to a friend in Florence. It was well I did so, for the letter directed to the Embassy apparently was intercepted, inasmuch, as when my friend called with the copy, the letter sent from me to the Embassy had not been received. Mr Eliot took up the case with earnestness and stated he would require an ample apology to me made by the Italian Gov. I have not yet received it, I shall wait a week and then if [it] does not come to hand, lay the case before Lord Clarendon.[72]

The weight of the responsibilities and some of the difficulties of his office weighed heavily on Polding's shoulders and at times he felt the strain. In July 1866 while at Blackheath, south-east of London he wrote in one of his many letters to HG Gregory:

> My dear Gregory, You will be surprised to find that I am still lingering about London. The fact is, I was nearly exhausted by the excessive heat of London, and the continued anxiety of my mind, reverting to what was done, and thinking that other arrangements would be better. I came out here on Friday last and have in some sort recovered the tone of my mind. But really I begin to fear I shall never be fit for much. This hesitation, this uncertainty and indecision grows upon me, and I have not much help in dear F. Edmund, though his will is stronger than his mind, and he sees too little before him as I, on the other hand, am inclined to see too much.[73]

In a further letter to Gregory in September of that year, Polding commented on his own outlook and a feeling of isolation. He was faced with some difficult issues in the Sydney church and felt he

72. Polding to B Smith, Belmont, 19 June 1866. *Polding Letters*, volume 3, 217–218.
73. Polding to HG Gregory, Bexley Lodge Blackheath, 17 July 1866. *Polding Letters*, volume 3, 221.

lacked support in Rome and elsewhere. Clearly Athy was not of the calibre required, helpful though he was.

> I am indeed very nervous and full of apprehension about the future. If I had someone with whom I could commune, but I have not. F. Edmund is not altogether the one I ought to have with me.[74]

Another thorn in Polding's side at this time was the repeated approaches from Athy's sister-in-law (Randal's wife) for him to be able to travel to Ireland to see his family. It was close to eleven years since Myles Athy had farewelled his family and sailed from Liverpool. Polding saw Athy's duties otherwise:

> No sooner have I got rid of one bugbear, but another rises up. The last is about F. Edm. I have had such reproaching letters from his Sister-in-law, about his not going over to Ireland, that I have been seeking for someone to accompany me so that I might leave him. Not but that I could go very well by myself, but this he will not hear of. The simple answer is that he came to be with me and not to see his frds. If he can, well and good, but not so as to interfere with the first object. Now this answer even in its politest form I cannot summon courage to give. [75]

Towards the end of that letter, Polding comments that he 'will start for Rome with or without a companion as we may agree'. It is unclear if Athy started out with him, but he was certainly with the Archbishop in Rome by November 1866. In a letter written while at the English College in Rome to Gregory he remarked on his and Edmund's puzzlement regarding the contents of a telegram from Gregory. 'I received on Saturday late your first Telegram, wh. puzzled me and Edmund not a little'.[76]

We do know that Athy eventually spent some time with family. Writing to Sr Scholastica Therry OSB in an undated letter, but thought

74. Polding to HG Gregory, Coll Inglese (English College, Rome), 12 September 1866. *Polding Letters*, volume 3, 249–250.
75. Polding to HG Gregory, London, 19 July 1866. *Polding Letters*, volume 3, 222.
76. Polding to HG Gregory, English College, Rome, 20 November 1866. *Polding Letters*, volume 3, 256–257.

to have been written in late 1866, Polding commented that 'F Edmd's only surviving Sister has just gone'.[77]

In a later piece of correspondence from Polding, written from Clapton (London) he wrote:

> F. Edm. will remain here with his Br. Randal, & Sister for some days, when the latter goes to the *Convt to enter the Convent, and the two former to Ireland.[78, 79]

We know from the English Census for 1861 that Athy's mother Bridget and his sisters Elizabeth and Catherine were all living in Hackney, London by that year. It is unknown just when they left Galway, as indeed, it is unknown when Myles Athy left Galway. The Athy women were companions and co-workers at Hackney with two other women, one the mother and the other the half-sister of a Father William Lockhart (22 August 1819–15 May 1892).

Elizabeth Athy died in 1863 at Hackney—almost three years before her brother was in London with Polding. Bridget Athy, Myles' mother died there on 7 February 1864 and it was Catherine, a member of a religious order, who was his 'only surviving sister'. She was a member of an order of Franciscan nuns and lived most of her religious life in a convent at Taunton in Somerset. She died there in 1911.

Father Lockhart was well known to Myles Athy; he is first mentioned in the journal entry for Friday 30 November, 1855 when he wrote:

> How I wish that dear F Lockhart was with us. I wonder whether I shall ever see him again. I wish that "The End of the World" would take it into his head to send him out. I am selfish enough for that, though I know how you would all howl.

77. Polding to Sr Scholastica Therry no address, c late 1866. *Polding Letters*, volume 3, 259–260.
78. Polding to HG Gregory, Clapton, London, 7 January 1867. *Polding Letters*, Volume 3, 261–262.
79. Br Terry Kavenagh, the Benedictine Brother who made me aware of the references to Athy in many of Polding's letters, held the view that this word may have been misread by the editors of the collection of the letters, taking it as meaning 'Convent' when perhaps it could have been 'Continent'. Presumably 'the two former' refers to Randal and his wife, although she is not specifically mentioned in this letter.

Only a week later, on his birthday, we read:

> And I reason that you were likewise praying for me, that on this my birthday[80] the grace of being born to a new life would be vouchsafed to me. I am very sure that the prayers of that little Angel Cat were offered also for me so that I am well provided with prayers. And what is of more value than all, the prayers of dear F Lockhart in his Mass.

Father William Lockhart IC: Connections close to home and heart

At the re-opening of St Etheldreda's Church in Ely Place, London after World War II, Monsignor Ronald Knox said of Father William Lockhart: 'He should be remembered for having provided one of the greatest passages in English literature. It was of him Newman was speaking when he preached his sermon on the Parting of Friends.'[81]

William Lockhart, was born on 22 August 1819 at Warlingham, Surrey, the son of Alexander Lockhart (c 1788–1831), a minister and high churchman of the Scotch Episcopalian school and his wife Martha (née Jacob, 1798–1872). Alexander Lockhart's first wife, Miss Carr-Newnes, had predeceased him. There was a daughter Elizabeth (1812–1870) from that marriage.

William was educated at Bedford Grammar School matriculating at Exeter College, Oxford in May 1838. By his own admission Lockhart's first year at Oxford was not confined to serious study, he whiled away some of his time with the boating and hunting set. However, he then settled into a more serious approach. He attended St Mary's University Church, where he heard sermons preached by John Henry Newman (1801–1890) who had been Vicar there since 1828. It was at this time that Lockhart was exposed to Froude's *Remains* and Faber's *Foreign Churches and Peoples*, material that awoke uncertainty in him about religious teachings that he had until then accepted completely.

By 1839, William Lockhart's widowed mother, Martha Lockhart, and her step-daughter Elizabeth were living in Chichester and attending the Cathedral there where the Archdeacon HE Manning

80. Athy was born 8 December 1818.
81. Nicholas Schofield, *William Lockhart, First Fruits of the Oxford Movement* (Leominster, Herefordshire: Graewing, 2011), x.

was based. They too had developed a deep interest in the Oxford Movement.

Lockhart wrestled with his doubts for some time. On the advice of Archdeacon Manning, he moved to Newman's small Christian community at Littlemore in July 1842 where he actually met Newman for the first time. At Littlemore, Lockhart continued his studies for the Anglican priesthood. In October of 1842 he met Aloysius Gentili, a Catholic priest of the Institute of Charity, a congregation established by Antonio Rosmini in 1828. This meeting was to influence Lockhart enormously. Rosmini's aim in establishing the Institute of Charity was to found a religious congregation which worked to perfect charity, which to him meant to perfect justice. He saw this as being achieved by discerning local needs but it could be carried out by preaching missions and retreats, running schools and colleges, publishing catholic literature or the pastoral care of parishes. The Institute established Ratcliffe College, Leicester in 1847.

Lockhart's exposure to Catholic teaching had created great doubts for him with regard to his Anglican convictions. Newman too, at this time, had to deal with his own doubts about the same matters. After much enquiry and discernment, Lockhart was received into the Catholic Church in August 1843 and a matter of days later was accepted into the novitiate of the Institute of Charity. Lockhart's conversion was the trigger for Newman's sermon 'The Parting of Friends'[82]. Newman resigned from Littlemore the following month. Lockhart went on to be ordained as a catholic priest of the Order of Charity in 1846.

Newman became a Catholic at Littlemore in October 1845, being received into the church by Dominic Barberi, a Passionist priest. He was ordained a catholic priest in Rome in 1847 and was created a Cardinal in 1879. He died in1890.

HE Manning (1808–1892) converted to Catholicism also. On 6 April 1851 he was received into the Catholic Church and a couple of

82. Joseph Gillow, *A Literary and Biographical History, or Bibliographical Dictionary of the English Catholics from the Breach with Rome, in 1534 to the Present Time*, 4 volumes (London: Burns & Oates, 1885–1902), volume 4, 303 to be found at <https://archive.org/search.php?query=A%20literary%20and%20biographical%20history%2c%20or%20bibliographical%20dictionary%2c%20of%20the%20English%20Catholics%20from%20the%20breach%20with%20Rome%20AND%20collection:toronto> Accessed 30 November 2014.

months later, on 14 June, he was ordained as a Catholic priest. In 1865 he was appointed Archbishop of Westminster.

Lockhart's mother became a Catholic in 1846, being received by Father Pagani of the Order of Charity at the convent at Loughborough. His half-sister Elizabeth followed in June 1848. The two women entered religion together; however, Martha Lockhart's health was not sufficiently robust and she had to leave religious life before making perpetual vows. In 1853 Elizabeth was professed under the religious name of Mary Elizabeth at the convent of the Third Order of St Francis near Glasgow. She later founded the Franciscan convent at Notting Hill and was its first abbess. The religious community ran a boarding school for young ladies and in 1868 opened St Elizabeth's Home, a home attached to the convent for the training of young girls as domestic servants. Elizabeth died in 1870.

Following his ordination, Lockhart assisted in preaching missions at Melton Mowbray and Loughborough. On 1 June 1847 he preached at the opening of the new oratory at Ratcliffe. A few days later he took up his appointment as curate at Shepshed in Leicestershire. At the same time he engaged in preaching in the open air in nearby villages. He was considered successful in this role and continued the work at various English towns.

In early 1851 Lockhart was sent to Ireland to preach at missions there and this time is said to have been most fruitful for his priestly work. Nicholas Schofield, in his book *William Lockhart, First Fruits of the Oxford Movement*, pointed out that preaching missions such as the ones undertaken by Lockhart were not necessarily aimed at catechizing the Irish poor but rather as a response to the proselytizing activities by Protestants who had been active in Ireland since early in the nineteenth century. The Protestants had intensified their efforts when the Famine struck in 1845, promoting the idea that the Famine was punishment being meted out to the Catholic Irish for their centuries of 'Romish' superstitions.

It is unknown when Athy and Lockhart's lives first intersected but it would be reasonable to speculate that they became acquainted on one of Lockhart's missionary assignments in Ireland in the early 1850s. Certainly the commitment of both families to a deep religious life was a common thread.

Lockhart was sent to Rome in late 1853. The following year he was appointed to Kingsland in London where he set to work establishing a house and church for the Institute of Charity. The name of Kingsland is not in common use in that part of London in the twenty-first century; it is in the area of Hackney and Islington in north London.

At the end of 1856, Martha Lockhart, accompanied by Catherine Athy, Myles' sister, moved from Greenwich to Kingsland so the older woman could be near her son[83]. Schofield writes that 'a house on Culford Road was rented by Mrs Lockhart and Miss Athy, who had also belonged to the Sisters of Charity of the Precious Blood at Greenwich. She was later joined by her sister and mother'.[84]

Martha Lockhart and Catherine Athy had settled into a convent-style arrangement nearby, wearing the religious habit. A school was established at Kingsland in January 1857. It catered for boys, girls and infants, each as a separate establishment. It is interesting to learn that the Headmaster of the middle-class boys' establishment, Joseph Atkinson, later combined his teaching duties with the editing of *Catholic Opinion*, a popular magazine that Mrs Lockhart purchased in the mid-1860s. In 1869 Atkinson left Kingsland to join the Rosminians. Mrs Lockhart's health failed her again and she had to leave the convent life for a second time late in 1857. The school was eventually taken over by the Sisters of Providence from Loughborough who were part of the Institute of Charity.

Martha Lockhart was a major benefactor in the establishment of her son's mission at Kingsland. Schofield writes that it seems she was quite involved in affairs there, helping with the housekeeping in the presbytery and having an advisory role of sorts.

The English Census of 1861 records Bridget Athy, her daughters Catherine Athy and Elizabeth Athy all living at Buckingham Road, Hackney. The same census records Martha Lockhart living at Culford Road. These two roads intersect, so the women lived in close proximity to each other. By 1861 Elizabeth Lockhart was the head of Franciscan Convent in Notting Hill, in the Borough of Kensington.

Father Joseph Costa, an assistant appointed to Kingsland in 1862, found the women's involvement in parish and clerical affairs to be quite interfering to the point where they were opening Lockhart's mail and acting like a religious superior in the house.[85]

83. Gillow, *A Literary and Biographical History*, volume 4, 297–307.
84. Schofield, *William Lockhart, First Fruits of the Oxford Movement*, 72.
85. Schofield, *William Lockhart, First Fruits of the Oxford Movement*, 72.

Archbishop Polding visited Lockhart at Kingsland during his trip to England and Europe in 1865-66.[86] Schofield wrote of the visit: 'Distinguished visitors to the parish included Archbishop Polding of Sydney, a friend of Lockhart's whose chaplain was a relation of Miss Athy, one of the schoolmistresses and companions of Mrs Lockhart'.[87]

The tone of another letter written by Polding to Gregory reinforces the notion of Polding and Lockhart being friends, as Polding sent Lockhart's regards to Gregory 'Lockhart & Mother desire all most kind—same in all manner of good wishes to self & the family'.[88] In 1859, Polding mentioned Lockhart's name in a letter to Bishop Goold who at that time was in Rome. In the letter he was proposing names for future bishops in various sees back in Australia. He proposed Bathurst as a destination for Lockhart and commented thus:

> I think Father Lockhart is precisely the man we want in Australia. He is a convert, it is true, but at the age of 23, and he is now about 40, seventeen years being spent in religion, full of energy, disinterested, equal to all exigencies; no priest is more valued by those who know him well. His letters are the emanation of a singularly gifted pious mind, withal so full of good practical common sense. I think he will be a treasure to the Diocese which possesses him.[89]

Nothing came of this suggestion.

Thirteen years later Lockhart's name again appeared, this time second in a list of three names that Polding offered to Archbishop HE Manning in 1872 as his preferences for the person to be appointed as his coadjutor in Sydney.[90] Roger Bede Vaughan was given that appointment.

During his years at Kingsland Lockhart suffered periods of ill health and he was moved to a less demanding role in the country air

---

86. Polding to HG Gregory, Bexley Lodge, Blackheath, 17 July 1866. *Polding Letters*, volume 3, 221.
87. Schofield, *William Lockhart, First Fruits of the Oxford Movement*, 83.
88. Polding to HG Gregory, St Scholastica's Clapton, 7 January 1867. *Polding Letters*, volume 3, 261–262.
89. Polding to Goold, Sydney, 11 February 1859. (Moran, 784–5) *Polding Letters*, volume 2, 268.
90. Polding to Manning, St Mary's Cathedral, Sydney, 31 December 1872. *Polding Letters*, volume 3, 363.

of Leicestershire between September 1864 and July 1865 where he acted as Vice-President of the Rosminian house at Ratcliffe College. He was accompanied by his mother.

By this time Martha Lockhart had turned her attention to the promotion of accessible Catholic literature. She bought two established publications, *Catholic Opinion* and the *Lamp*. She established St Joseph's Press, a printing office near Fleet Street and devoted her energies and not inconsiderable wealth during her remaining years to that end. Father Lockhart was also involved in the editing and publishing of these magazines and during his lifetime also wrote or edited many other works, translating some works of the founder of the Institute of Charity, Rosmini.[91]

Martha Lockhart died at Kingsland on 15 January 1872 and was interred in the Cemetery of Ratcliffe College, where she had been a special benefactor.

In 1873 Father Lockhart was sent to serve in the very poor area of Holborn in central London. In December of that year the ancient Chapel of St Etheldreda's in Ely Place, an historic thirteenth century building which had been closed to Catholic worship since the time of Henry VIII was to be sold. He arranged for its purchase and set about restoring it. Five years later Mass was celebrated in the building for the first time in over 200 years. St Etheldreda's is still a vibrant Catholic Parish to this day.

During his years at Ely Place, Lockhart worked with the Temperance Movement, regularly spent months at a time in Rome working for the Rosminians, continued his preaching around England, and directed religious retreats for various religious communities and seminaries.

Lockhart had maintained a close relationship with Newman all his life and mourned his passing in August 1890. Another major figure in Lockhart's life, Cardinal Manning died in January 1892. Lockhart died suddenly at Ely Place on 15 May 1892.

Schofield writes that Lockhart was considered for appointment as Bishop in a variety of places over many years. Polding's proposals have already been mentioned, but there were proposals to appoint him to Nottingham, England in 1874, to Lanarkshire in Scotland in 1878, to the Archdiocese of St Andrews, Scotland in 1884 and in the final year

91. For full list of publications, see list in Gillow, *A Literary and Biographical History,* volume 4, 297–307.

of his life there were strong rumours that he would be appointed as Coadjutor of the Archdiocese of Westminster.[92]

Lockhart had no ambition for higher office, at one time writing to Cardinal Manning 'Thank God I shall never be a bishop'.[93] At the time the rumours were circulating of a possible appointment to St Andrews in 1884, Lockhart wrote to Manning, trying to persuade him to intervene. The Cardinal refused, saying 'I shall not send the letter to Scotland nor in any way cross what may be God's will. If He chooses you it will be, if not it will not be, and if it be, He will give you all needful from health to Canon Law'.[94] Lockhart was mightily relieved when another was named for the position.

Lockhart's activities had a profile in Sydney. An article in the *Freeman's Journal* of 20 May 1876 referred to him as 'one of the best-known priests in England'.[95] The *Freeman's Journal* had published an excerpt from his 'Lectures on the Catholic Religion' in 1865,[96] Lockhart's account of his mother's conversion in 1872[97] and the newspaper also commented on Lockhart's response to an item in the *Dublin Review* in 1876[98].

The closing lines of Schofield's biography state: 'William Lockhart was buried in the (Ratcliffe) college cemetery, beside his mother and the Athys.'[99]

It would seem Bridget and Elizabeth Athy's final resting place was the cemetery at Ratcliffe.

92. Gillow, *A Literary and Biographical History,* 151–153.
93. Gillow, *A Literary and Biographical History,* 151.
94. Gillow, *A Literary and Biographical History,* 152.
95. 'An English Catholic on Irish Home Rule', in *Freeman's Journal*, 20 May 1876, 5.
96. 'The Rise of Christian Rome', in *Freeman's Journal*, 8 March 1865, 147.
97. 'An Account of Mrs. Lockart's (sic) Conversion', in *Freeman's Journal*, 27 April 1872, 4.
98. 'Father Lockhart and the Dublin Review', in *Freeman's Journal*, 3 June 1876, 13–14.
99. Nicholas Schofield, *William Lockhart, First Fruits of the Oxford Movement*, 157.

Athy's later years

Following the long visit to Europe and England, Polding and Athy arrived back in Sydney in August 1867. They had sailed on the *Chariot of Fame* from Liverpool, and spent a few days in Melbourne before Athy boarded the *City of Adelaide* to arrive in Sydney on August 3; Polding followed four days later on the *Alexandra*.

The question of leadership of the Benedictine Community in Sydney was a constant concern for Polding. While still in England, and writing to Gregory about, among other things, the apparent lack of good leadership within that Community, Polding expressed his view that 'the case of the Benedictines is almost hopeless. There are some fine young men, and F Edmund would be found a valuable aid, but a head is wanting.'[100]

On a similar theme, Polding wrote from Sydney to Gregory In 1871:

> Something might be done in the way of resuscitating the Benedictine soul and body. What can I do? I have not one who is thorough. Father Edmund Athy would be useful under a proper Superior, but you know he is always sugar! Thoughtless.[101]

Father Athy served on the teaching staff at Lyndhurst for a time. Lyndhurst comprised a boys' school and Benedictine Seminary in

100. Polding to HG Gregory, English College, Rome, 17 November 1866, *Polding Letters*, volume 3, 255–256.
101. Polding to HG Gregory, Sydney, 6 October 1871, *Polding Letters*, volume 3, 351–352.

Glebe overlooking Blackwattle Swamp (now Wentworth Park). The school was established by Archbishop Polding first at his residence at Woolloomooloo and called St Mary's College, and it was then moved to the Cathedral. Polding initiated the purchase of Lyndhurst in 1853 and the College was transferred there. The Novitiate for the formation of Benedictine religious was moved to Lyndhurst in July 1857. Lyndhurst was closed in mid 1877 by Polding's successor, Archbishop Roger Bede Vaughan OSB (1834–1883), a matter of months after Polding's death.

A former pupil at Lyndhurst, John Lane Mullins wrote an article describing certain aspects of Lyndhurst during his years as a school student. Mullins (1857-1939) was a pupil from 1868 to 1873 inclusive. He later graduated from the University of Sydney and worked as a barrister. He emerged as a Catholic lay leader, served in a variety of elected positions in Government and exhibited great generosity to the community in general. He wrote the article in 1933.

> The College grounds embraced many acres and fronted on the northern side the water then known as Blackwattle Bay, and since reclaimed and now the reserve of Wentworth Park.
>
> The Benedictine community resided in a large and fairly commodious mansion of two stories with a large stone verandah in front and cellars below. The view from the verandah disclosed Johnstons Bay in the near distance. There was a circular drive to give access and exit. A spacious grass plot was enclosed by the drive and in its very centre a huge fig-tree decorated the landscape, and well tended flower beds and handsome umbrageous trees flanked the drive and decorated the community grounds. A huge eagle belonging to Father Edmund Athy OSB was chained under the shade of the fig tree. Out in a westerly direction the garden extended towards Bridge Road. In spring all this meadow land lit up with the variegated blooms of ixias, sparaxis and the beautiful coloured tints of the babiana and other spring bulbs.[102]

102. Hon Lane-Mullins, John. MA, MLC *Manly, Journal of St Patrick's Seminary,* 'Memories of Lyndhurst', 1933, 63.

After his work at Lyndhurst, Athy continued to serve in the Sydney area. In December 1872, the *Evening News* reported on a Solemn High Christmas Mass celebrated at Mount Carmel Church at Waterloo. It would seem Father Athy was held in high esteem:

> After the conclusion of mass, a very eloquent and instructive sermon on the festival celebrated was given by the parish priest, the Rev. Father Athy. Judging from the extraordinary progress made by this church since it has been under the direction of the present clergyman it seems now in a position to rank with almost any of the Catholic churches in the city or suburbs.[103]

Athy also undertook parochial work in Haymarket prior to the overseas trip in 1865[104] and again in 1877,[105] at St Benedict's at Broadway[106] (1873), at Brisbane Water[107] (1874) and at Bulli in the Illawarra area.[108] (1881.) The church at which he served in Haymarket was St Francis de Sales. It was built in 1864 on the corner of Campbell and Elizabeth Streets on land that had to be resumed in 1908 for the construction of Central Railway. The church buildings were demolished in 1909.

There are conflicting records of Athy's appointments in the 1880s. According to John Fletcher's *A Chronicle 1877–1977*, Athy was appointed in 1880 as assistant to Father John Pollard (c 1847–1884), the first Parish Priest of Forest Lodge and that he remained until 1887. However, at the blessing and opening of the new Catholic Church at Bulli in September 1881, Father Athy was referred to as 'pastor of the district'.[109]

In January 1882, the *Illawarra Mercury* reported:

> We understand that the Rev. E. Athy has been appointed by His Grace the Archbishop as Priest of the Parish of Wollongong,

103. 'News of the Day', in *Evening News*, 31 December 1872, 2.
104. 'St Francis Church', in *Freeman's Journal* 8 March 1865, 148, 149.
105. 'The Archdiocese', in *Freeman's Journal*, 10 November 1877, 14.
106. 'Parochial Changes', in *Freeman's Journal*, 15 February 1873, 10.
107. 'Clerical Changes', in *Freeman's Journal*, 31 January 1874, 10.
108. 'St Patrick's Church', in *Freeman's Journal*, 17 September 1881, 15, 16.
109. Fletcher, John, *St James' Church Forest Lodge, A Chronicle, 1877 –1977*, 4.

> which includes Bulli and Coal-Cliff. It is also understood that the Rev. Father O'Donohoe is to assist Father Athy, whose genial manners and other good qualities have rendered him quite popular since his arrival in this district.[110]

In July 1882 the *Freeman's Journal* recorded that 'we understand that a priest will be shortly appointed to assist Father Athy at Wollongong'.[111] October 27 of that same year, ME Athy was the signatory to an advertisement in the *Illawarra Mercury* to notify the public of the Mass times at St Francis Xavier's Church in Wollongong (8 o'clock) and St Joseph's Church, Bulli (at 11 o'clock).[112]

In December 1882 Athy dislocated his shoulder and collarbone after his horse stumbled and fell while he was riding from Bulli to Wollongong. The writer of the article in the *Wollongong Argus*, which was reprinted in the *Freeman's Journal* suggested:

> We should imagine, that the parishioners of the reverend gentleman would avail themselves of the unfortunate accident to procure for him a buggy, which for a man at his time of life and who is always visiting among his flock would be a graceful and handsome testimonial to a clergyman, who since his advent to the district has been so zealous in carrying out his clerical duties. We trust this suggestion may be acted upon, feeling certain its accomplishment will depend on its initiation.[113]

By December 1883 Athy was back at Forest Lodge as assistant to Father Hugh Callachor, who had been appointed Parish Priest in December 1882. Father Athy's health apparently began to deteriorate, as on 24 October 1885 Dr O'Haran wrote to Cardinal Moran (Archbishop of Sydney 1884-1911) 'poor Father Athy is breaking down, unable to do his duty'.[114] Father Athy was sixty-six years of age at this time.

---

110. 'Roman Catholic', in *The Illawarra Mercury,* 13 January 1882, 4.
111. '*St Vincent's Convent*', in *Freeman's Journal*, 15 July 1882, 16.
112. 'Advertising', in *The Illawarra Mercury*, 27 October 1882, 2.
113. 'Catholic', in *Freeman's Journal*, 9 December 1882, 8.
114. John Fletcher, *St James' Church Forest Lodge, A Chronicle, 1877–1977,* 6.

He left Forest Lodge in early 1891, retiring to the care of the Patrician Brothers at St Charles' Villa, Home for Aged and Invalid Priests at Ryde.[115] 'Father Athy is one of our oldest priests, and at St Charles' Home he will have the companionship of another venerable priest of the diocese, the Very Rev. Dr. Hallinan.'[116] He passed away on 19 October 1891 at the age of 72. His Requiem Mass was celebrated at St Charles' and he was interred at Field of Mars Cemetery, Sydney.[117]

A few weeks later, Athy's worldly affairs were being finalised, as the following notice in the *Sydney Morning Herald* indicated. It is interesting to note that one of the solicitors in the firm handling his affairs is named Makinson. Athy referred to H Makinson in his journal.[118]

---

115. A Bit of History, *Green Sash* V 12, 13 July 2005, 379–380.
116. 'Clerical Appointments', in *Freeman's Journal*, 14 February 1891, 14.
117. 'Death of Rev ME Athy One of the Old Benedictines', *Freeman's Journal*, 24 October 1891, 14.
118. On board the Phoenix was Thomas Cooper Makinson (1809–1893), his wife Sarah Ann (née Soulby, 1815–1873) and their children, the eldest of whom, Henry was born 1840 in Sydney.
Thomas Cooper Makinson was ordained a priest of the Church of England in the Manchester area of England in 1836 before marrying Sarah in 1837. He worked as a curate at St Ann's Manchester. He responded to the call for clergy to serve in the new colony and emigrated to Australia. He arrived in Sydney in January 1838 with his wife of less than twelve months on board the *Siam* and commenced parish work at Mulgoa, also serving the South Creek area.
The rise of the Oxford Movement had an impact on Makinson, to the extent that he, along with a fellow Anglican clergyman, Robert Sconce, were received into the Catholic church by Archbishop Polding in February 1848. Polding gave Makinson and Sconce employment as teachers at a lay school attached to St Mary's Seminary and Makinson was also on the teaching staff at St Mary's Lyndhurst, overlooking Blackwattle Bay in Glebe.
In 1854 Makinson, his wife and children, went to Liège in Belgium, where Makinson worked as a tutor. Around this time Polding appointed him as his Secretary and so he returned to Australia on board the *Phoenix* in the company of the Archbishop and the group of Benedictines including, Myles Athy. Makinson remained in his role as Secretary to Polding until the Archbishop's death in 1877. With his eyesight now failing, Makinson was allowed a pension by Polding's successor, Roger Bede Vaughan. He lived out his final years in Gladesville, dying in 1893. His wife predeceased him, having died in 1873.
Henry Makinson, the youth to whom Athy referred in his Journal, taught for a time at Lyndhurst in his adult years and later established a legal firm in Sydney. He died in 1913.

IN THE SUPREME COURT OF NEW SOUTH WALES.—PROBATE JURISDICTION.
In the Will of the Reverend MYLES EDMUND ATHY, late of Sydney, in the colony of New South Wales, Clerk in Holy Orders, deceased.

APPLICATION will be made after fourteen days from the publication hereof that Probate of the last Will of the abovenamed deceased may be granted to the Reverend BERNARD CALLACHOR, the sole executor named in the said will.

Dated this 29th day of October, A.D. 1891.

ELLIS, MAKINSON, and PLUNKETT,
Proctors for the said Executor,
49 Elizabeth-street, Sydney. [119]

By any measure, Myles Athy was a minor player in the latter half of the first century of Catholic life in Sydney. He was a loyal travelling companion, sounding board and at times a carer for Archbishop Polding over a number of years. As we have gleaned from Polding's comments, the Archbishop felt that Athy did not have the talent to rise to great heights in the administration of Benedictine affairs in Sydney. Polding dearly wished that such a person was at hand. Certainly Athy would have wildly exceeded his mother's expectations for him, keeping in mind her comments to Father Brown when Myles was a sixteen-year-old student at Downside. As for the people he ministered to in his adopted land, contemporaneous material suggests that he was widely loved and respected, a man who worked hard in the field to which he was allocated. He had great faith in his God.

> 'All who knew the good, kindly, generous-hearted priest will think of him now that he is gone with affectionate regret.'[120]

Bishop Batallion: A Marist Missionary in the Oceanic Region

Athy's final resting place is but a few kilometres from the head of Tarban Creek, where he had come ashore on his recreation day excursion in late 1856 during his first year at St Mary's Monastery. This outing was the subject of his comments in the final pages of the journal.

---

119. *The Sydney Morning Herald*, 30 October 1891, 114.
120. 'Death of Rev ME Athy One of the Old Benedictines', in *Freeman's Journal*, 24 October 1891, 14.

The French Bishop to whom Athy referred in this journal entry was Pierre Bataillon, a man who spent forty years working as a Marist missionary in the region of Oceania.

The growth of the Catholic Church in Australia, the Pacific and Oceanic regions is inevitably intertwined. The role of the Marist's and Bataillon's involvement in it is a story of commitment, tragedies, strong personalities and a drive to help the word of God take root in these places, far from the familiar comforts of the missionaries' homes.

Pierre Maria Bataillon (1810–1877) was born 6 January 1810 in Saint-Cyr-les-Vignes, a small village about 500 kilometres south-east of Paris in the Loire Department, France. He was ordained a priest on 19 December 1835.

More than twenty years earlier, in 1812, a young seminarian Jean-Claude Courveille (1787–1866) was at a Marian sanctuary at Le Puy in Velay, France when he felt inspired to found a religious community dedicated to work in missions. The Society of Mary (members of the Order are generally referred to as Marists) was formed in 1816 when several young priests and seminarians at the diocesan seminary in Lyon vowed to found such a group. Pope Gregory XVI granted Papal Approbation on 29 April 1836 following the commitment of the newly formed congregation to undertake the missionary work in Western Oceania in the South Pacific. Jean-Claude Colin (1790–1875) was elected the first Superior General of the order.[121]

In May 1836 Jean-Baptiste Pompallier (1801–1871) was consecrated Bishop and appointed the first Vicar Apostolic of the newly formed vicariate of Western Oceania. It was a vast, triangular shaped area, about 8,000 kilometres from east to west and as far from its northernmost point to the southern edge, straddling both the equator and the Tropic of Capricorn. It took in New Zealand at its southernmost point, all of New Guinea, north as far as the Marianas Islands, and east to include Samoa, known then as the Navigators Archipelago, Tonga, Nuie Islands, the Mangaia Archipelago and all the island groups in between.[122]

---

121. <http://www.maristsm.org/en/history.aspx> Accessed 6 April 2015.
122. Ralph Wiltgen, *The Founding of the Roman Catholic Church in Oceania 1825 to 1850* (Canberra: ANU Press, 1979), 127.

On Christmas Eve 1836, under Pompallier's leadership, the first group of Marist missionaries comprising four priests and three Brothers left Le Havre, France, on board the *Delphine* bound for Valparaíso, Chile. From Chile the group planned to then sail to their mission field. Pierre Bataillon and also Pierre Chanel (1803–1841, later canonised) were amongst their number.

Following his ordination, Bataillon had served as a diocesan priest in Lyon and volunteered to join the group at the last minute. He was directly invited by the vicar general of the Lyon archdiocese, Father Jean Cholleton. Cholleton knew the priests who were forming the Marists from their days in the seminary where he had been the professor of moral theology. He later joined the fledgling order himself.[123]

Bataillon arrived at Wallis Island (Uvea) on 1 November 1837 to commence his work amongst the population of about 3000 people. He was now twenty-seven years old and had with him Brother Joseph-Xavier Luzy, a fellow Marist and carpenter who was to also work as a catechist. Chanel, along with Brother Marie-Nizier Delorme was allocated the island of Futuna (Horn), about 190 kilometres south west of Wallis. Pompallier began work in New Zealand.[124]

The Marists, under Superior General Colin, continued to send workers to Oceania. By early 1841 over forty priests and brothers had left France to work in the vast area.

On 23 August 1842 Bataillon was appointed the Vicar Apostolic to Central Oceania, based in Tonga. He was ordained Bishop in 1843. This new vicariate apostolic was carved out of the vicariate of Western Oceania and included the Wallis Islands, Futuna Island—where Chanel had been martyred in 1841, archipelagoes of Tonga, Fiji and Samoa as well as New Caledonia and New Hebrides. Bataillon later estimated that he had charge of a population of six hundred thousand souls at that time.

It was by any definition an isolated and harsh life. The tyranny of distance, irregular visits by sailing vessels and difficult communications had to be endured. Oceania was the first mission field outside France in which the Marists undertook work. Indeed,

123. Hosie, *Challenge*, 9–13.

124. Wiltgen, *The Founding of the Roman Catholic Church in Oceania 1825 to 1850*, 158.

being a new congregation, it was their first missionary venture, their commitment to missionary work being the basis of the new order's Papal Approbation. In August 1859 the *Freeman's Journal* published an unattributed report that was apparently written by Father Victor Poupinel, the relatively newly appointed visitor general and procurator general to the Marists in Sydney. It noted that at that time sixty two priests and thirty-four catechists were working in the Pacific Ocean area. At the time of the report, seventeen priests and eight lay brothers had already died in the course of their work, either by shipwreck, falling victim to illness or murder 'by the savages. Three, and probably six, have been eaten by these cannibals'.[125]

A decision to establish a procure house in Sydney for the Marists had been made by Superior General Colin in 1844, with the agreement of Archbishop Polding, himself an ardent missionary, in order to support the scattered Marists in the Oceania region. The relationship between the Sydney Marists and Polding was, at times, quite difficult. John Hosie's *Challenge: The Marists in Colonial Australia* deals with the interactions between the French priests and the first Catholic Bishop and later Archbishop of Sydney in some depth.

Beverley Sherry writes in her entry 'Hunters Hill' in the *Dictionary of Sydney*:

> In 1847 the Marists purchased a house at Hunters Hill as a place to keep their stores and as a rest and recuperation centre for their missionaries; they named it *Villa Maria*. The Marist Fathers sold the house in 1864, moved to Mary Street, and transferred the name *Villa Maria* to the stone monastery and church they built there. The original stone house, now known as *The Priory*, still stands at the head of Tarban Creek. In the 1870s, the Marist Brothers joined the Fathers in Hunters Hill and established their school, St Joseph's College on Ryde Road. The school building, constructed over a period of time from 1882–1904, is one of the finest sandstone buildings in the suburb. The French Marist Sisters also came to Hunters Hill and in 1908 established a high school for girls on Woolwich Road.[126]

125. 'The Society of Mary', in *Freeman's Journal*, 27 August 1859, 2.
126. <http://www.dictionaryofsydney.org/entry/entry/hunters_hill> Accessed 25 April 2015.

Bataillon was able to visit Sydney from time to time and was much respected by the people there. He arrived, along with some natives of Wallis Island on the *Henri* on 8 May 1852.[127] A few weeks later, on Sunday May 30, nine Wallis Islanders received their First communion in St Mary's Cathedral.[128] Around this time some of the islanders staying at the Marists' house in Sydney were also engaged in quarrying sandstone from Pyrmont for the churches on Wallis and Samoa as an article published some years later reveals:

> The principal station of these missions—the place where Monsignor the Vicar-Apostolic would reside did not circumstances require his continual travel—is at Apia, an island of the Navigator's Group, where there is a Catholic church built of stone from our Pyrmont quarries. Old residents in Sydney will remember how, some ten years since, Dr Bataillon and a number of natives whom he had brought up from the islands were for some time employed in quarrying and preparing the stone near Lyndhurst.[129]

Bataillon took part in celebrating Archbishop Polding's eighteenth anniversary of his consecration as archbishop by officiating at Benediction on 29 June 1852 at St Mary's.[130] The Marist missionaries had the support of Sydney Catholics who rallied to help following the shipwreck of the supply vessel, *Spec* (*Speculator*), an incident that saw the loss of goods that were bound for the various mission stations in the Oceania region.[131] A relief fund was set up and substantial subscriptions were raised.[132] As well as generous donations from Sydneysiders to support the missionary effort, other inventive ideas were used to raise funds, including:

---

127. <http://mariners.records.nsw.gov.au/1852/05/007hen.htm> Accessed 8 May 2015.
128. 'St Marys Cathedral', in *Freeman's Journal*, 3 June 1852, 10.
129. 'Departure of Catholic Missionaries for the South Seas', in *Freeman's Journal*, 28 May 1859, 2.
130. 'Eighteenth Anniversary of His Grace the Archbishop', in *Freeman's Journal*, 24 June 1852, 10.
131. 'Loss of the Spec. Bishop Bataillon', in *Freeman's Journal*, 5 May 1855, 10.
132. Hosie, *Challenge*, 103.

Just Published, price 1s. 6d.,

AN Excellent PORTRAIT of the RIGHT REV. PETER BATAILLON D.D., Catholic Bishop of Oceanica.

The proceeds of this Engraving are devoted to the furtherance of the Mission for the Conversion of the Natives of the Southern Pacific.

To be had at the Office of the FREEMAN'S JOURNAL, and at Mr. Dalton's, George-street. [133]

It was during one of his visits to Sydney in early 1856 that Bataillon was at the Marists' house near Tarban Creek for some months while he printed material in the language of the people in his mission. He left for Europe in May of that year. Athy indicates in his journal entry that he had seen Bataillon sometime after his own arrival in Sydney in January of 1856. The building to which Athy refers is probably the structure that is now called *The Priory* and can be accessed off Salter Street, Hunters Hill.

In 1859 the enthusiasm and commitment of Sydney Catholics to assisting the missions was unabated:

HIS GRACE the Archbishop of Sydney directs a COLLECTION to be made in all the Churches of Sydney, on SUNDAY MORNING next, the 5th instant, in aid of MONSIGNEUR BATAILLON, whose mission has unexpectedly met with a very heavy pecuniary loss. [134]

It was said of Bataillon that he 'enjoyed exceptional success as a missionary. Bataillon cut an impressive figure with his long beard, his forthright approach, and the sheer force of his personality. Bataillon made great demands on himself and his missionaries, who paid a high price in exhaustion and isolation'.[135]

As with all human endeavours, differing opinions, differing methods of performing a task and personality clashes are part and parcel of life. The exacerbation of certain personal eccentricities

133. See *Freeman's Journal*, 11 November 1852, 1. (no title).
134. *The Sydney Morning Herald*, 3 June 1859, 1. advertising.
135. <http://www.acertainway.info/on-mission/setting-out/any-part-of-the-world> Accessed 26 January 2015.

as one ages can occur, and if accompanied by a lack of insight into one's behaviour, significant problems can develop. The life of a catholic missionary priest was no different. Bataillon's reputed strong personality and style of leadership brought him into conflict with those in his charge, with fellow bishops and with his superiors, both within the Marist congregation and at the Vatican.[136]

For some years Bataillon had been contemplating the idea of establishing a college in Sydney to house and educate promising young islander men from his vicariate and hopefully see some of them enter the priesthood. He had established a college-seminary in 1847 at Lano on Wallis (Island) to that end. He was hoping that the young men of promise would undertake studies to become catechists and perhaps some would go on to study for the priesthood.[137] In moving the house of studies to Sydney, part of his thinking was that to remove the students from their local environment and install them in a monastic setting would help their spiritual formation. At one point he had hoped to establish it at the Marist house, *Villa Maria*. Unfortunately Bataillon's style was that such an arrangement would see the house transition from being a facility for all the Marists in the region to something over which he had complete control and would use for his own purposes, albeit missionary purposes.[138] In 1859 Bataillon bought a thousand hectare property on the Cumberland Plain, about forty-eight kilometres west of Sydney, called *Clydesdale*. It was situated on South Creek, a tributary of the Hawkesbury River. His vision was grand: not only would it be an educational institution but also a farm, growing wheat, and grapes for winemaking. The proximity of the site to the river system was part of the undoing of the grand plan. It was flooded many times during the 1860's.

By early 1860 there were probably twenty students there. Three returned home when Bataillon found them unsuitable, others joined the group, and by the end of 1864 there were twenty-seven in residence. Following a series of floods in the area, thirteen of the students were returned to the islands. Over time the men who had come to *Clydesdale* for their education found themselves undertaking heavy manual work to develop and maintain the farming aspect of

136. Ralph Wiltgen, *The Founding of the Roman Catholic Church in Melanesia and Micronesia, 1850–1875* (Eugene Oregon: Pickwick Publishing, 2007), 429–458.
137. Hosie, *Challenge*, 108.
138. Hosie, *Challenge*, 170.

the facility. Discontent developed amongst both the staff and the students. The experiment at *Clydesdale* was unravelling. As Hosie wrote:

> The effect of this loneliness and isolation on normally gregarious and easy-going Polynesians can be imagined. They were earnest young men, who had sincerely embraced Christianity, and desired to take a further step of dedication to Christ, even if one assumes that they were somewhat vague about the details of this step. To have come such an unimaginable distance from their small home islands was already a strain. Add to these problems the monastic discipline then regarded as essential for the education of priests, lengthy times of required silence, extremely long hours of classes in obscure sciences, tiring manual work, with night study by candle light, and a penetrating winter cold never experienced in their islands.[139]

The combined effects of these pressures and the alien cultural expectations that were imposed on the men resulted in the failure of the project. By 1869 the college was being wound down and the property was sold in 1871.

Following the closure of *Clydesdale*, Bataillon reopened the seminary at Lano, on Wallis, in an attempt to provide an avenue for local men to pursue a vocation to the priesthood, should they so wish.[140] Four Wallisians began studies there in 1874 and would go on to be ordained in 1886. Bataillon's idea of a self-supporting and indigenous Catholic church in the Pacific was beginning to bear fruit.

Around the same time as the *Clydesdale* purchase, Bataillon also bought a ship, renamed *Caroline*, to enable his easy movement around his vicariate and back and forth to Sydney. The vessel was refitted at Sydney before undertaking her first voyage under Bataillon's ownership on 27 May 1859.[141] Heavy costs of repairs and other running costs saw it sold just three years later at a financial loss.[142]

139. Hosie, *Challenge*, 179.
140. Hosie, *Challenge*, 182.
141. 'Departure of the Catholic Missionaries for the South Seas', in *Freeman's Journal*, 28 May 1959, 2.
142. Hosie, *Challenge*, 172.

In 1863, a fellow Marist, Father Louis-André Elloy (1829–1878), who had been serving under Bataillon since 1856, was ordained Bishop and appointed coadjutor to Bataillon in Central Oceania.[143] Bataillon's strong-mindedness and possibly fears of losing control of certain parts of his vicariate contributed to an extremely difficult relationship with the newly ordained bishop which saw Cardinal Prefect Barnabo, who headed *Propaganda Fide* (that part of the Vatican hierarchy responsible for the Propagation of the Faith), intervene in an attempt to find a solution satisfactory to both Elloy and Bataillon as well as the Vatican. The unhappy situation dragged on for years. In February 1870 Barnabo asked Bataillon to come to Rome so the conflicted matters could be resolved. In spite of several follow-up letters, Bataillon remained in Oceania. It was not until October of 1871 that he eventually left Wallis for Sydney, and sailed from Sydney for Europe in February of 1872. He was in Rome when, after a series of exchanges with Barnabo, and in consultation with Father Julien Favre (1812–1885) the Superior General of the Marists based in Lyon, France, a solution was thrashed out. In May 1854, at the age of forty-one, Favre had succeeded the founder and first Superior General of the order, Father Jean-Claude Colin. The new arrangement with Bataillon provided for the Navigators Archipelago to be separated from Bataillon's Central Oceania vicariate and given to his coadjutor, Bishop Elloy to administer it as its Pro-Vicar Apostolic. The difficulties between Elloy and Bataillon had run for nine years.

In August 1875 Bataillon submitted a report to Rome about his vicariate. He wrote that his Central Oceania vicariate had once been 'very vast, but today is one of the smallest vicariates in Oceania because the vicariates of New Caledonia, Fiji and Samoa, have all been separated from it'. His Central Oceania vicariate consisted of 'groups of islands, of which the principal ones are Uvea [or Wallis], Futuna, Rotuma, Tonga, Haapoi, Vava'u and Tokelau. We have mission station on all of these islands, but we do not yet have missionaries to send to other less important islands.' He wrote that the Roman Catholic religion 'is flourishing most of all on the island of Uvea or Wallis. For this reason it is called the Little Rome of Oceania.' It was here thirty-three years ago that the Catholic religion was first implanted and it

143. Wiltgen, *The Founding of the Roman Catholic Church in Melanesia and Micronesia, 1850–1875*, 429.

was from here that it spread to the multitude of islands which were then still part of the Central Oceania vicariate. 'The Church of Uvea' Bataillon said 'which I with the help of God had the consolation of founding, now numbers more than one hundred encircling daughter churches. This is a very consoling result and one that has been achieved in the space of thirty years.'[144]

Unfortunately Bataillon did not live to see the fruits of his labours with the ordinations of students from Lano in 1886, he had died in 1877 on Wallis.

As Hosie wrote of Bataillon: 'In another age, one has no difficulty visualising him leading troops into battle, like a Pope Julius II. But despite his dictatorial leadership, he had incredible drive and determination. Without him, the Marist missionary endeavour might have been brought to stagnation and defeat.' He continued: 'Bataillon's far-sighted vision of the Catholic church, self supporting and indigenous to the Pacific, was the only basis on which it would survive in the long term.'[145]

There is an image of Bataillon depicted in a stained glass window in the Catholic Church in Lapaha, Tonga.[146]

144. Wiltgen, *The Founding of the Roman Catholic Church in Melanesia and Micronesia*, 482, 483.
145. Hosie, *Challenge*, 185.
146. <http://apifoou.com/apifoougallery/displayimage.php?album=41&pos=29> Accessed 26 April 2015.

29 ✱ Nov.

Saturday 10th Rose at 6-20 - Morning very fine - a few clouds. Wind S.E. by E. Course S.W. by S. All sails, save Mizen Main & [illegible], set Ship's rate of going 7 Knots per hour - M.P. Study 8-15 - 9-30 Breakfast - Fare. Broiled ham. Bacon and Liver - Curry - Potatoes boiled - Cold Tongue - (Salt being cold) Rice. Stirabout. Bread & Ship biscuits butter. Onions raw - Tea - 10.0. on deck Ship astern of us approaching - All sails set Studsails Main & Fore - Awning on deck As we are in the Tropics the heat is on the increase - 11.30 1-45 Studying - 1 P. Lat 22.28. Eighteen degrees within the ~~Tropics~~ Tropics - Long. between 19.20 - Lunch did not partake of it - Very Very Very hot 2 1/2. 4 Confessions Thank Our Lord I have been to Confession and to, I trust that tomorrow I shall have the unspeakable happiness of receiving into my breast Him who has brought me here - May He by His grace instruct and enlighten me 4. 0. Heave the Log rate of sailing 6 1/2 Knots per The Vessel that had been following us is now taking another course she is a brig - It is many

1855

Journal kept on the Voyage to Sydney Australia on board the Ship *Phoenix*

By Myles Athy

Saturday October 27

The Archbishop[147] came on board at about $6^{H}.0^{M}$. Weighed anchor at about $7^{H}.0^{M}$. Were towed down the Mersey by the tug steamboat Dreadnought which parted from us at $11^{H}.20^{M}$ as the wind was fair. Fresh breeze blowing. Weather a fair wind.

At about $11^{H}.40^{M}$ Mr Livingstone, one of the owners, I believe, who came out with us from Liverpool, an agent, an extra carpenter, and a nondescript all of whom were with us, parted from us and returned to Liverpool by tug steamer dreadnought. We gave three cheers on their departure.[148]

Ship's Horary.[149] Breakfast $9^{H}.0^{M}$, Lunch $1^{H}.30^{M}$. Hove the log.[150] Sailing before wind 10 miles per hour. The table not so full to day owing to the rolling of the ship which had an uncomfortable effect on some of our mess mates.

Definitions without attribution are from *Webster's New International Dictionary*, Second Edition 1934.

Information and guidance on Liturgical matters was provided by Fr Colin Fowler OP.

147. 'Archbishop' is Archbishop John Bede Polding OSB, (1794-1877) See p 7 Athy Biography for more information.
148. In the Journal, Athy has inserted this sentence between lines of writing. I have placed it at the end of the paragraph where it makes most sense.
149. 'Horary' is an account proceeding by hours.
150. 'Hove the log'. A log line is used to measure the rate of a vessel's motion. Each knot on the line bears the same proportion to a mile that twenty eight seconds do to an hour. The number of knots which run off the reel in twenty eight seconds therefore shows the number of miles the vessel is sailing per hour. Thus when a ship goes eight nautical miles per hour her speed is eight knots.

4^{H}. Dinner. The table to day was very thinly attended as the rolling of the ship had taken effect on the health of some of our mates. As yet I am pretty well able to eat my dinner and smoke my pipe.

5^{H}. Abreast of Holyhead. Here sad thoughts came to my mind of those dear ones I have left behind and whom I hardly dare hope to see again in this world. We have had some years of happiness together and now our lot is to be separated and our happy family circle broken up.

May the Will of the Most High be done is my continual aspiration when my heart is sad.

Our dear Archbishop has not appeared since morning.

Supper 8^{H}. Sick list increased.

The weather has cleared up. A bright moonlight night, but unfortunately the breeze towards 11^{H} has fallen so that we are not making much way at least not as much as one could wish. M.A. [*Athy initialled this entry*]

Sunday Oct 28

Very fine weather, breeze very light. Bkft about 9^{H}.

Prayers read to day by Dr Gregory[151]. Acts, Psalter, Litany BVM[152] Manner of hearing Mass Gold. Man.[153] Mass was not celebrated to day. The Archbishop still continues sea sick. Some of our messmates who were sick yesterday made their appearance to day looking particularly seedy, some at Breakfast & others at Noon. The time was taken to day. At about Noon were abreast of some rocks off the Welsh coast called the "Bishop & his Chicks". We shall not see the coast of Ireland, as we have kept along the Welsh coast to take advantage of the wind of which at present there is very little. The sun prognosticates southerly wind & rain. I dare say we shall have rain tonight.

We have sighted some 7 or 8 ships to day up to 12^{H}.O.

---

151. See p 18 Athy Biography for information on Gregory.
152. 'BVM' is abbreviation for the Blessed Virgin Mary. The Little Office of Our Lady is a liturgical devotion of the Catholic Church. It is a cycle of psalms, scripture readings and hymns that are in addition to the Divine Office, the official Prayer of the Church.
153. The Golden Manual is a guide to Catholic devotion, both public and private.

Since 11^{H} we have had a perfect calm, the more unpleasant as we are in the vicinity of some ugly looking rocks, off the Welsh coast, called the Smalls.

Went forward amongst the forecastle passengers, a rum looking set they are, being a motley crew. Amongst them are some Germans with their fraus. These are the dirtiest of the whole lot. I had a talk with a young Irish man from the County Cork who with six or seven others, is on his way to the diggins. He told me that he had no need to go as his father is a farmer holding 200 acres of land under Lord Bantry;[154] but somehow or other his mind has been for the last three years bent on going to Australia, so he could not rest easy at home, he is a quiet lad of about, as well as I can judge, 20, or 21 years of age. I shall have more talk with him yet.

Yesterday I heard a lady of our party congratulating herself and others that there were no smokers of our party. Which same egregious mistake I did not care to contradict. I believe that she is nearly on the same errand as I am, as I understand she is to join the Benedictine community her name is a Miss Adamson.[155] I gave a wink to one who knows I smoked and laughed in my sleeve. I laughed or rather smiled as I think that she suspected, as she added, "at least if any one does smoke it must be on the sly".

Really to day is just like a summer's day every one almost except our dear Archbishop being sitting on deck; some reading, some talking, others walking about and others like myself doing nothing particular.

---

154. Lord Bantry was a landholder in the south of Ireland, west of Cork. His actions, involving evictions of tenants and his dealings with a landowner to whom he sold some of his property makes for interesting reading, see http://www.irishidentity.com/stories/bearaevictions.htm Accessed 7 May 2015. http://archiver.rootsweb.ancestry.com/th/read/Beara/2012-07/1342058156 Accessed 7 May 2015

155. Miss Mary Ann Adamson was a young woman travelling with some professed Benedictine Nuns who were on their way from St Mary's Abbey, Princethorpe in Warwickshire, England and bound for Sydney where they were to join their monastery, 'Subiaco' near present day Rydalmere. Miss Adamson was destined to enter the Sisters of the Good Shepherd, a religious order of nuns that Archbishop Polding was establishing. The order later changed its name to the Sisters of the Good Samaritan and Sister Magdalen, as Miss Adamson's professed name became, would be the first elected Superior General of the order. (This information supplied by Sister Lia Van Haren, Archivist of the Sisters of the Good Samaritan, Glebe Point, NSW.)

About $3^{H}.30^{M}$ a slight breeze sprung up which brought us away from the Islands off the Welsh coast called the Smalls on one of which there is a lighthouse erected on the top of some piles. We had been for two hours during the calm drifting steadily down upon them. The captain himself told me that he feared we should drift on them unless a breeze sprung up.

The breeze lasted for about 2 or three hours and then fell away again, and up to this hour $10^{H}.15^{M}$ there has been a perfect calm, not a ripple on the sea, the night very bright and we are drifting back again until we have got abreast of the Smalls. Several porpoises have been swimming about, and one grouping has been quite close to the ship. I hope that before morning a breeze may spring up, otherwise we may find ourselves ashore somewhere.

Went to bed at about $12^{H}.45^{M}$. The lights of the Smalls look unpleasantly near but a nice breeze has now sprung up and is carrying us away from them.

Monday Oct 29

I rose this morning at $8^{H}.20^{M}$. Breakfast $9^{H}.30^{M}$. Saw several ships. Weather rather too calm we are making but little way. We have had a glimpse at Irish land in the distance. N.E. by N. I suppose that it is the coast of [*left blank*].

Two of our messmates again indisposed.

I shall commence a letter today as it is possible we may drop in with some boat off the Irish coast to take it off and should I not succeed I can keep it till I can get a chance of sending it. Alas! All hope of speaking either ship or boat has vanished, we have lost sight of land.

$1^{H}.30^{M}$. Luncheon. I did not go down to this meal today. Before dinner I went to see the Archbishp who is somewhat better today.

$4^{H}.0^{M}$. Dinner. After dinner went on deck. There was a considerable swell setting in. Remained on deck till $11^{H}.10^{M}$ by this time the swell had greatly increased, and promised a rough night.

$11^{H}.30^{M}$. Went to bed, but could not sleep as the rolling of the ship made all the timbers creak which made so much row that it was useless to attempt to sleep.

Tuesday Oct 30th

This morning there is a tremendous sea running. The vessel is rolling & pitching at a fearful rate. Crockery ware thrown off the shelves and smashed, it is with difficulty that we can keep in our beds. When we can get up on deck I expect we shall see some grand waves.

$7^{H}.0^{M}$. Went on deck, to see the waves. Really I cannot describe their magnificence.

Mountains of water seemed to be in motion and were knocking us about like a shuttlecock it is with the greatest difficulty one can keep one's legs. I have had no less than three falls already.

$9^{H}.30^{M}$. Breakfast. I was for sometime anxiously waiting for this meal as I felt only so, and I knew that breakfast would set me all right.

Wind N. E. Ship's bearing W.S.W.

In the Atlantic Ocean. And a true Atlantic swell we are in. Twice during lunch was the table nearly turned over, and all of us to maintain our seats had to hold on like grim death. As for the deck it is quite a feat to walk without falling even while I am writing these lines it is with considerable difficulty that I can keep my seat on the deal box in my cabin.[156]

There goes something crash next door.

The entire ship is creaking & groaning. The only fear the Skipper has, that we may lose our masts.

There have been porpoises playing about the ship, and various wild looking sea-fowl some of which I think are of the petrel kind indeed I think most of them are. I fear that the gale which has now sprung up will not go down to night so we shall have another unpleasant night of it.

We had great fun to day on deck endeavouring to walk on a single plank and failed I think scarcely more than one or two succeeded.

The waves are still very high and the wind is rising. Some of our mates are sick again & I am just beginning to feel rather unpleasant, if this swell does not soon go down I fear that it will be all up with me.

Dinner about $4^{H}.0^{M}$. Went up on deck did not feel very comfortable. Came down sat in the Cabin read office Vespers B.V.M & Rosary. Sat in saloon some were playing at chess others reading.

---

156. A 'deal box' is made of unfinished timber, usually pine or fir. Deal timber is generally plain, unfinished wood.

6^{H}. Went in to read to the Archbishp Chapter on Penance. Ah how beautiful it is the colloquy between Xt and Man so full of consolation and so expressive of contrition.

$7^{H}.30^{M}$. Tea. After Tea went on deck, sat there with F Keatinge till prayers were announced.

$8^{H}.30^{M}$. Prayers. Went on deck again H Makinson came with me. [157] The night was very dark and blowing a whole gale of wind from N.E. Ship rolling fearfully Course S.W. by W. Six sails set and all double reefed. Smoked two cigars on the seat next the door.[158] Retired at $11^{H}.0^{M}$.

Wednesday 31st

Rose $6^{H}.30^{M}$. Ship still rolling but the gale is subsiding. Feel very uncomfortable I am very nearly sick, I hope I may hold on.

Bkfst $9^{H}.30^{M}$. Fasting 'not binding' at sea. Capital bkfst, Ham & Eggs. Chops etc. Did not eat any. Feel excessively seedy today, have to lie down several times. Took some camphor dissolved in rectified spirits of wine, a mixture given me by the doctor instead of spirits of camphor for which I asked. After bkfst sauntered on deck for a while then went to lie down and say office B.V.M in my cabin, did not go to lunch not feeling inclined to eat anything. Rather sick so could not do anything but wander from one place to another seeking rest.

$4^{H}.20$. Dinner. After which I recovered somewhat. The wind & sea have gone down very much. So much the better for me as I now have a chance of escaping sickness. Went up to see a Cow which is sick. Saw her given Chatswood. & Parkinson.[159] I felt so done up that I was obliged to put off concluding this day's journal till 1st Nov.

Went down to Saloon played a game of Whist; F Keating and I against F McGirr and W. Makinson.[160] The second game I had to get

157. See p 47 Athy Biography for more information.
158. This is as written in the Journal, probably meant 'next **to** the door'.
159. This appears to be what is written here, but just what is being referred to is unknown. One reading of the script is that Athy went to visit a sick cow and that it was given some medication called 'Chatswood and Parkinson'. It has not been possible to discover anything to prove or disprove this theory.
160. Rev F McGirr appears to be 'McGees' in the passenger list at Sydney, see: http://mariners.records.nsw.gov.au/1856/01/scan.asp?filename=085pho.gif Accessed 20 May 2016.

F Mellitus to take my place, having to go and read pecksniff to the Archbishop.[161] Chapter for Wednesday, "Paradise of the Soul". This was after tea.

Night prayers.

Went on deck, smoked a cigar & pipe. Night very fair breeze rather light, a lazy sort of swell that makes the ship roll. Went to bed at $12^{H}.0^{M}$. The whole of today we have been crossing the entrance of bay of Biscay.

November

Thursday 1st

All Saints
Rose at $8^{H}.30^{M}$. Fine weather. Wind N.E. course S.W. by W. Stunsails set.[162] Heard that we spoke the Schooner [*left blank*] bound for L'pool this morning at about 8^{H}. Unfortunately I was not up so I lost the chance of sending home a letter.

Bkfst $9^{H}.30^{M}$. After bkfst said M.L. and little hours of BVM.[163] At about $11^{H}.0^{M}$ Dr Gregory read prayers. Mass for the absent from Golden Manual, 2 Part Psalter. Litany of Saints. I suppose the Ship rolling so much prevented our having Mass.

Saw a barque in the distance ahead of us all the morn. Holding the same course as us. At about $1^{H}.0^{M}$ we overhauled and spoke her.

---

161. Seth Pecksniff was a major character in Dickens' *Martin Chuzzlewit*. This is not to say that Athy was reading Dickens to the Archbishop but rather that he may be using 'Pecksniff' as an expression of a sentiment he had about the activity he was undertaking with the Archbishop. See Appendix I p 159.
162. 'Stunsails'. In light winds studding sails (pronounced "stunsls") may be carried on either side of any or all of the square rigged sails except royals and skysails. They are used to increase the sail area of a square rigged vessel They are named after the adjacent sail and the side of the vessel on which they are set, for example *main topgallant starboard stu'nsail*. One or more spritsails may also be set on booms set athwart and below the bowsprit.
163. 'Matins and Lauds' are Prayers of the Divine Office, the official prayer of the Catholic Church. Matins and Lauds are usually prayed at sunrise. Others are Vigil, prayed at night, Prime, at 6am (first hour), Terce at 9am (third hour), Sext at noon (sixth hour), None at 3pm (ninth hour), Vespers is the evening prayer at sunset and Compline is prayed before retiring for the night. The Psalms, Scripture readings and other prayers form the Office.

The *Calphurnia* from Glasgow bound to Madras. No passengers she appeared rather heavily laden. Passed her about $1^{H}.15^{M}$.

2.45. Went to the Archbishop's cabin to read. A beautiful chapter it was in the "Paradise of the Soul" of a Thursday "On Holy Communion".

That man nondescript of "soi-disant" BA of Trinity College was decked out today in a most fantastic fashion, something á la "Giaour" in Byron.[164, 165, 166, 167] In the evening he wore a Greek cap with two or three tassels dangling from it. They say that by profession he is an attorney but judging from his cut I should think him better adapted for the diggins than the law. All the passengers were lounging about the decks today the weather being so fine.

Course of vessel S.W.

$7^{H}.30$. Office for the Dead. Played at whist after tea. To bed at $11^{H}.45^{M}$.

Friday 2nd

Rose at $7^{H}.30^{M}$. Said morn prayers and M & L BVM.

$9^{H}.15^{M}$. Breakfast. Fare: boiled Ling, Sardines, Mashed Ling & potatoes, Boiled Potatoes. Curried fowl, Hot rolls, rather black but pretty good. Ship biscuits, Tea & Coffee. I tried the boiled Ling but had to send it away. I did not like it, not being "the best". After breakfast sauntered on deck till $11^{H}.0$. This is the time for seeing geniuses[168] as they generally "turn out" between 10^{H} & 11^{H} there is one on board. The nondescript "Giaour". I ought not to dignify him even with the title of Giaour. "That Tumbler" would be more á propos. He wears a blue Guernsey shirt, no neck tie, a flare up Greek cap with a couple

164. A 'Nondescript' is a person or thing not easily classified belonging, or apparently belonging, to no particular class or kind; usually applied disparagingly. An oddity.
165. 'Soi-disant' is an adjective, meaning so-called, would-be, pretended, supposed, allied, seeming, self styled.
166. Trinity College is a Protestant University in Dublin.
167. 'Giaour' is a Turkish expression to describe an unbeliever or infidel (in Muslim eyes) usually a Christian. It is a derogatory term. Lord Byron wrote a poem with the title 'The Giaour'.
168. 'Geniuses' can mean a peculiar character or being (from an earlier meaning as a spirit or being).

of tassels dangling therefrom, like folly with the fool's cap and bells, on his head. I got in chat with him once, but then he was equipped in a national costume so I did not examine him much. I think that at some time I shall take his measure.

11^{H}. Prayers for the dead read by Dr Gregory. These lasted for about half an hour. When finished some of us employed the time reading others walking on deck. Some saying office till about 12^{H} when luncheon was announced of which those that felt inclined partook. After lunch, indeed the whole morning, a bark[169] was seen to the Eastward of us steering the same course. Likewise a homeward bound Schooner crossed our bows within half a mile.

The weather today is very fine though now the sky is a little overcast and happily the breeze has freshened. Hove the log. Ship's rate of sailing seven and half knots per hour. Wind [*left blank*]. Course S.W. by W.

I forgot to remark that in the morn we were all sorry to hear that the Cow was very unwell having refused her food. But later in the day seven bottles of gruel were given her after which she rallied & took some food.

Our Friend the "Street Swell" in consequence of a change of temperature, had to modify somewhat the airy costume in which he appeared this morning. He doffed his Greek head gear and replaced it with a national cap, provided his neck with a tie. I forgot to mention that a day or two ago this same wight displayed his agility in climbing to the cross tree of the mizzen, to the admiration of his fellow passengers and for which he had to pay dearly; for as soon as he got up, a few Jacks followed him and told him that he must pay his farthing. He refused, upon which they seized him and bound him to the ladder and left him there, till punished in his elevated position, he agreed to pay 5^{s}-6. Upon which they let him down.[170]

It just served him right. I thought that I had described this fellow in the first or second pages of these notes; as I find not, I shall just say that a day or so after we started one of the party got into conversation with him when he said that he was a B.A. of Trinity College, had tried to get a place in our cabin, but could not succeed so as he wanted particularly to go at once he took a berth with the steerage passengers

169. 'Bark'. A barque, a type of sailing ship.
170. 'Wight' is a preternatural being, a fairy; a creature.

2 Class. By the bye he came over from Dublin on the same night with Randal and in the same steamer.[171] He came 1st Class in the steamer so R must have seen him. I think I have written this before but no matter.

Well to resume, the breeze freshened nicely this A.M. and drove us 11 or 12 knots per hour. I went to read to the Archbishp just before dinner. No abstinence today.

We are now off Portugal from which we are distant about 150 miles.

Dinner today about 4^{H}.30^{M}. Tea 7^{H}.0^{M}.

I am writing this in my cabin at night all the others are some playing cards others draughts & chess. I have been reading Russell's "War".[172] I shall now shut up and take a turn on deck it is a little after 9^{H}.0, about 8^{H}.30^{M} of your time.

11^{H}.25^{M}. Very stormy.

Saturday 3rd

Rose at 7^{H}.20^{M}. Prayers and Office before Bkfst. Went on deck to read office.

Bkfst 9^{H}.30^{M}. Tea, Chops, Curry & c. After Breakfast spent some time reading 'The War' and other things, some of which were peckSniff.

Good News. Dr Gregory is preparing the Altar for Mass tomorrow. How refreshing it will be. I hope that we may be permitted to approach the "Most Holy". To receive Him whose Word the Strong Winds fulfil, and at whose Will the angry waves arise, and subside again. What an awful happiness would it be. The manner in which the Chalice is secured, is by a piece of wood one end of which embraces the lower part of the cross the other the stem of the Chalice, in such a manner as to permit of the Chalice being elevated without its being detached from its safeguard thus [*here an illustration*].

---

171. Randal Athy was the writer's brother. In the next sentence he is referred to as 'R'.
172. William Howard Russell (1820-1907) was an Irish-born war correspondent for *The Times*, the prominent English newspaper. His reporting from some theatres of the Crimean War (October 1853 to February 1856) brought the savagery, inhumanity and tragedy of war to the attention of the British public. His writing was acknowledged by Florence Nightingale to have been the stimulus for her entry into wartime nursing. Amongst other works, he published the two Volume work 'The War' 1855 & 1856 on the Crimean War.

1^{H}. Lunch. Of which I did not partake.

Got into chat with the B.A Trin Coll. Found that he is a Meath man, whose Uncle is Rector of Moate. Says that his brother-in-law has a share in a property in Australia worth 16,000 per annum. I suppose that this wight is being sent out to superintend it. He appears to be a liberal chap enough. Says that his Uncle cannot endure the Muggletonians with which Moate swarms, but that he is hail fellow well met with the Catholic priests and especially with the Abbot of some Monastery there.[173] He, the B.A., also always enquires after the Archbishop asking how is "His Grace". So perhaps he is a better fellow after all than he appears; but his fantastic costume makes him look odd.

Went down to read in my cabin. Afterwards at about $2^{H}.30^{M}$ read to the Archbishop then went to Dinner at $4^{H}.0^{M}$ or thereabouts. Fare: Mutton boiled. Fowl. Curry. Ham. Vegetable. Entrée. Tarts.

Walked on deck, smoked a Pipe. Went to cabin to prepare for Confession.

Tea at $7^{H}.30^{M}$. Marmalade. Butter. Biscuits & Bread.

$8^{H}.10^{M}$. Went to confession to the Archbishop. Oh what a comfort to get one's conscience scrubbed up again after a fortnight's rusting. For in the bustle of starting and amidst the times of sea-sickness I did not like to try to go. So I waited till things got somewhat into ship shape. No Communion tomorrow. All things not being as yet prepared. Weather all today has been fine. Breeze rather light from the S. Course S.W. by S. Bed $11^{H}.45^{M}$.

Sunday 4th

Rose at $6^{H}.45^{M}$. To be in time for the Holy Sacrifice which is to be offered at $8^{H}.0^{M}$. Office B V M on deck.

---

173. 'Muggletonians' were members of a small, almost extinct Protestant Christian sec that was established in 1651. It was led by two tailors, Lodowicke Muggleton (1609-1698) and John Reeve (1608-1658) who believed they had been commissioned by God. Other similar groups included the Ranters, the Seekers and the Quakers. T.L. Underwood. *The Acts of the Witnesses*. New York. 1999. https://books.google.com.au/books?id=o2NMCAAAQBAJ&pg=PP1&lpg=PP1&dq=Underwood+'Acts+of+the+Witnesses'&source=bl&ots=QkC1ADGXxn&sig=-pfvBr7Jhp2nHr10nqUvfDplPGk&hl=en&sa=X&ved=0CDIQ6AEwBGoVChMI2NaPnIyPyAIVwpOUCh21vQJv#v=onepage&q=Underwood%20'Acts%20of%20the%20Witnesses'&f=false Accessed 24 September 2015.

8^{H}. Mass, at which we had a good congregation from the forecastle, principally Irish. Dr Gregory celebrated. Today feels somewhat like Sunday. One feels less like an infidel after being sprinkled as it were with the blood of the Spotless Lamb. May God be thanked for His great mercy in sending me in this Ship. It is such an unspeakable blessing.

Bkfst at $10^{H}.0^{M}$.

$11^{H}.30^{M}$. Prayers from Golden Manual and a chapter from Imitation.[174]

$1^{H}.0^{M}$. Lunch. Saw three ships in the offing all outward bound. A small but beautiful kind of gull came flying close to us to day from which I infer we are not very far from some land though none can be seen. Since Monday we have not seen land.

We are to have Mass on other days this week I am glad to say.

In the afternoon overtook and passed four ships outward bound. The evening was exceedingly soft and mild. I staid on deck till just 12^{H} admiring the beauty of the stars for I never saw them so beautifully clear as they are in these latitudes. And there is not the slightest coolness. I could stop on deck till 12^{H} with only one coat on, and that a dress coat. There were two or three stormy Petrels following in our wake today.

Monday 5

12^{H}. Latitude 34 S.[175] Course S.W. by S. Wind S.S.E.

Rose at $7^{H}.30^{M}$. Prayers and Breakfast as usual. Saw some ships in the offing. Almost all sails set, and nice breeze. Commenced reading Latin with the Archbishop, Paradisus Animae.[176]

1^{H}. Lunch. Afterwards heaving by in the morning 9¾ knots and evening about 8 knots per hour.[177]

At $4^{H}.30^{M}$ sighted Madeira about 34 miles from us very indistinctly. After dinner at about 7.30 lost sight of it.

---

174. *Imitation of Christ* by Thomas à Kempis is a Christian devotional book first composed in Latin ca. 1418–1427. It was for many centuries the most widely read devotional work after the Bible.

175. As he is still off Portugal, 'S' is incorrect. Madeira is 32 N.

176. *Paradisus Anime Intelligentis* is the Latin name of a book, a collection of German language sermons, many written by Meister Eckhart from the fourteenth century. The title translated is *Paradise of the Intelligent Soul.*

177. 'Heaving'. Thus the crew were using the knot rope to measure the nautical speed of the vessel.

Fine mild evening and night. Staid on deck till nearly 12. The watch descried at $10^{H}.30^{M}$ a light on our lee bow.[178] He also burned three lights from our side, one each time. We passed her, she proved to be a brig outward bound.

F. Newman made his appearance on deck to day, he is much better, but he has had a severe attack of sea sickness. To day is very close. I wish I had a thermometer.

Tuesday 6th

Rose at 8^{H}. Office & Bkfst.

Afterwards went on deck. Ship going about 4 or 5 knots per hour. All the passengers were on deck today and truly the intermediate and steerage wanted the air to purify them for a dirtier looking set one could scarcely imagine.[179] There was rather a bit of a sea last night, much to the discomfort of some of those who had been sick already as it brought on a relapse.

Entered into talk with the Methodist chap. He is a coach maker by trade going to Geelong to set up there.

I must try and get the Latitude, Longitude and distances of each day since we started. Saw one or two ships in [*the*] offing. A Stormy Petrel was following us to day.

Tea 7.30. Smoked a pipe on deck.

Retired to rest at 11^{H} 0. A dead calm to night not a breath to stir the sails, here we lie in mid ocean just heaving about with the swell.

Wednesday 7

Rose at $8^{H}.15^{M}$. There is a fresh breeze blowing from N. E. Going about 6 or 7 knots. Latitude [*left blank*] Longitude [*blank*]

Every one on deck to day it seems to be a washing day with the emigrants as sundry portions of apparel are hanging about the ship. And dirty specimens of clothing they are.

Breakfast at 9.30. Fare: Salt Ling boiled, Mashed ling which is very good, a little broiled ham.

178. 'Descried' means to spy out or discover by the eye an object distant or obscure.

179. There were 250 intermediate and steerage class passengers on *Phoenix* when it arrived in Melbourne according to a report in the Shipping Intelligence column of the Melbourne newspaper the *Argus* of 19 January 1856.

After breakfast went on deck remained there for about three quarters of an hour smoked a pipe; then came down and wrote the exercise, from the Paradisus Animae, which was given me by His Grace. Said some of the office BVM and made a meditation. Up on deck again at 12^{H}. Ship had all sails set, going fine.

1^{H} Lunch.

$1^{H}.45^{M}$. To His Grace's cabin to read the exercise, read also another portion of Paradisus in English to him and then chapter in Bible. The exercise given me by His Grace being to translate part of a section in Paradisus Animae.

4^{H}. Went on deck again. Ship had all sails set going 8½ knots per hour. Father Newman came up to day he is very weak, he suffered from sea sickness. The holy Nuns were on deck likewise, one of whom also suffered severely. She appears very weak.

In the morning there were some showers. There was a bark before us part of the day but we overtook and gave her the go by. She appeared to be an English vessel, she had lost her top gallan yard.[180]

Tea at $7^{H}.30^{M}$. Afterwards some played whist others were reading, and some were on deck. I went on deck to have a quiet pipe.

Dr. Gregory is the life and soul of our party, he is so cheerful and full of fun, he often has us in roars of laughter. It is delightful to have him with us rather for us to be with him.

To day ginger beer was produced for me thanks to Bartholomew, His Grace's servant, a Galway lad, he went to the head steward and got it for me.

Night prayers at $8^{H}.50^{M}$. After which there is loitering about, and punch for those who choose it. I am at a great loss being a tee-totaller. I lose wine and punch every day.

This horrid lid of this box, has just fallen whilst I was looking for something and scraped my nose and face. I shall be a nice figure.

Thursday 8th

Rose at $7^{H}.10^{M}$. M. Prayers. Writing translation.

180. On a square rigged sailing vessel, a topgallant sail is the square-rigged sail or sails immediately above the topsail. In Athy's text the final 't' does not appear to have been written, but it is quite possible that this is the sail to which he refers.

Bkfst $9^{H}.30^{M}$. Fare: Chops. Ham & Liver. Curry and Hash. Potatoes, these every day & Tea. Hot bread, very black, & Biscuits.

On deck at $10^{H}.0^{M}$. Weather very fine. Wind very light, N.E. Course S.S.W. All sails set save the Mizzen, Main and the Bowsprit sails Lat 26.56, Long 19.30. The day will be fearfully hot it is now only $11^{H}.0^{M}$ and I can scarcely bear it. A vessel in the offing.

11^{H}. I came to my cabin to write the exercise given by His Grace; by the bye he gave me a little cross for my cabin this morning.

Rate of sailing 5 knots per hour.

$2^{H}.30^{M}$. Very heavy shower lasted for about 15 or 20 minutes rain fell in buckets full.

$1^{H}.45^{M}$. Went to read to His Grace as usual. Wind at $3^{H}.15$ N.N.E.

$4^{H}.30^{M}$. Dinner. Soup. Fare: Roast Mutton. Boiled Turkey. Ham. Sheep's head & Trotters. Curry. Vegetables, Potatoes, Turnips, Carrotts.[181] Rice boiled. Puddings, Plum & Sago, Sweet Raisins, Figs, Nuts.

6^{H}. Heaved the Log. Rate of sailing 4½ knots.

We had a very fine sunset this evening but I have seen finer at Renville.[182] But as soon as the sun had set the sea assumed the most beautiful tint I ever beheld. It was a perfect indigo.

They say that we shall soon see the flying fish. We had the Stunsails and some of the Trysails set today besides the ordinary sails.

To rest $11^{H}.0^{M}$.

Great laughing at me for having my face so scratched. Everybody remarking and asking me if I looked in the glass.

Friday 9th

Rose $6^{H}.20^{M}$. M. P.[183] I was shockingly slow this morning as I did not get on deck till $8^{H}.10^{M}$. But this is to be said there was no water in my jug and I could not procure any for a long time. The morning was superb such a clear air. Ship had all sails set. Course S.S.W. Wind light N.N.E. Rate between 6 & 7 knots per hour. I said all sails set. I was wrong. I must except the Mizzen, Main also the bowsprit sails.

181. 'Carrotts' is as spelt in Journal.
182. Athy was born at Renville, County Galway, Ireland, and spent some of his early years there.
183. Probably abbreviation for Morning Prayers.

10^{H}. Awning stretched over the quarter deck for the first time. Played a game at draughts with F Newman.

$11^{H}.15^{M}$. Down to prepare translation.

12^{H}. Lunch. Did not partake. Reading in Cabin.

Lat 24.46 Long betwixt 19 - 20. Course S.S.W. Rate [*blank*].

I forgot to give the bill of Fare from Breakfast so better later than never, here it is. Boiled Ling. Pickled Salmon (cold). Mashed Ling. Potatoes. Rice. Curry, and something else, I could not make out what, Bread (stale), Ship biscuit, Tea etc. The day is warm but there is a nice little breeze.

$1^{H}.45^{M}$. Went to read to the Archbishop.

$3^{H}.15^{M}$. Spare time on deck.

$4^{H}.30^{M}$. Dinner. Fare: Pork, roast. Fowl. Tongue. Mashed Ling. Pickled Salmon. Vegetables, Potatoes, Cabbage of course. Dumplings & Sago Puddings. Wines, Port & Sherry every day.

In the afternoon the Skysails and Royal stunsails were set. Rate of sailing from 5 to 6½ knots per hour. Breeze being light. Saw a ship in the offing astern.

$7^{H}.15^{M}$. Tea. Bread. Biscuits and preserves.

$8^{H}.0^{M}$. Some played Whist. The remainder of us were on deck.

9^{H}. Night prayers.

$9^{H}.30$. Punch.

$11^{H}.30^{M}$. Rest.

Saturday 10th

Rose at $6^{H}.20^{M}$. Morning very fine, a few clouds. Wind S.E. by E. Course S.W. by S. All sails, save Mizzen, Main and bowsprit, set. Ship's rate of going 7 knots per hour. M. P.

Study $8^{H}.15^{M}$.

9.30. Breakfast, Fare: Boiled ham. Bacon and Liver. Curry. Potatoes boiled. Cold Tongue, Salt Herring cold, Rice. Stirabout. Bread, stale. Ship biscuits, butter. Onions raw, Tea.

$10^{H}. 0^{M}$. On deck. Ship astern of us approaching. All sails set, Stunsails, Main and Fore. Awning over deck. As we are in the Tropics the heat is on the increase.

11^{H} to $1^{H}.15^{M}$. Studying.

12^{H}. Lat 22.28 being two degrees within the Tropics. Long between 19 – 20.

Lunch, did not partake of it. Very, Very, Very hot.

2^{H} – 4^{H}. Confessions. Thank Our Lord I have been to confession and I trust that tomorrow I shall have the unspeakable happiness of receiving into my heart Him, who has brought me here. May He by His grace instruct and enlighten me.

$4^{H}.0^{M}$. Heaved the log rate of sailing 6½ knots per hour. The Vessel that had being following us is now taking another course. She is a brig. It is nearly dinner time so I shall shut up for the present.

$4^{H}.30^{M}$. Dinner. Mutton Roast. Boiled Corn Beef. Fowl. Bacon. Some kind of Pie. Curry. Stew. The Archbishop had something, I am sure I don't know what, before him. Potatoes, Roast. Cabbage. Turnip. Carrotts. Puddings – Sago & Rice. Tarts, preserved plums & cherry. Wines, Port & Sherry. Beer & Porter.

After dinner the breeze was very light. There was a very pretty sunset. As yet I have seen none equal to the sunsets of dear old Renville, tropical though these are.

$7^{H}.0$. Rate 5½ knots.

$7^{H}.30$. Tea. After tea I went on deck smoked a little and meditated somewhat on the approaching delights of tomorrow.

9. Rate 6 ½ knots.

$11^{H}.20^{M}$. Rest.

Sunday 11th

$6^{H}.30^{M}$. Rose and set about, immediately after washing, to prepare my miserable house as a habitation for Him, "Whom my soul loveth". Alas! With how cold a love.

Mass $8^{H}.0^{M}$. Our dear Archbishop officiated, how delightful it was to hear again his well known voice in the August Mysteries. I brought sad recollections to my mind however for it was the same voice which sound years ago in the Holy Mass at which I made my "First Communion".[184] Alas how different was the Myles Athy of that happy day from the same person of Sunday 11 November 1855. Then comparatively speaking my heart was pure. Ah through what an abyss of evil has it passed since. May He who lovest all things, whatever He

184. Myles Athy likely received the Sacrament of First Communion during his school years at Downside (1831-1837). Polding was teaching there at the time. See H N. Birt. *Benedictine Pioneers in Australia,* London 1911, Volume II, p 325.

has made, recreate, for nothing else will do it, it must be an act of Omnipotence, in me the spirit I have lost, and clothe it again with the wedding garment I then at least not very long after cast away.

One feels renovated today. A lot of us have been to "Holy Communion". What a difference it makes. One feels as if one had some chance now of keeping the Sunday as one should. Thank God for having vouchsafed to visit his servants on the "Great deep". All His own deep. "For even the winds and the sea obey Him". Blessed for ever be His Sacred Name. I thought of all you dear ones this morning I hope that you did not forget me. It seems at such times as if we were not so far asunder after all for we are walking in the One House, and feeding at the same Heavenly Table, on That Bread which cometh down from Heaven.

After Mass and Thanksgiving, Breakfast. Fare: Chops. Broiled Ham and Eggs. Roast Potatoes – sliced. Curry. Cold corn beef. Stirabout. Bread stale. Ship Biscuit. Butter. Tea.

$10^{H}.30^{M}$. Went on deck. All sails set. Running fine course W.S.W.[185]

Wind [*blank space*] Rate of going at 11^{H} 7½ knots. Breeze pretty nice.

12^{H}. Lat 20 1m Long 20.

Lunch. Cold Corn Beef. Yarmouth bloater eaten raw which by the bye are very nice.[186] Biscuits & Cheese. Beer & Porter. Wines, Port & Sherry.

Just before Lunch we had prayers read in English by Dr. Gregory after which went our way till dinner. At $3^{H}.15^{M}$ I went to read Scripture to His Grace and had a talk with him afterwards.

Dinner $4^{H}.30^{M}$. Fare: Curry. Soup. Boiled Leg Mutton. Fowl, Boiled. Ducks steamed. Boiled Tongue. Irish Stew. Curry. Fowl. I believe. Veg. Potatoes. Cabbage. Turnip & Carrotts. Porter & Ale. Wines. Port & Sherry. Self G Beer.[187]

185. Word 'fine' difficult to read, this seems most likely.

186. Bloaters are a smoked herring. They are salted and lightly smoked without gutting, and are particularly associated with Great Yarmouth, England, thus 'Yarmouth' Bloater. They were popular in the 19th and early 20th centuries. The name "bloater" derives from the fact that they swell during preparation. See: http://www.information-britain.co.uk/food/foodlegends/Bloaters/ http://deptfordpudding.com/tag/bloater/ https://en.wikipedia.org/wiki/Bloater_(herring) Accessed 20 May 2016.

187. G.B.: Being Ginger Beer for himself.

Rate of sailing varying from 5½ knots to 7 knots.

A misfortune happened to me to day.[188]

They say that Flying Fish have been seen.

7^{H}.30^{M}. Tea. Jam. Biscuits. Bread. Preserves. I forgot a course dinner - kind of Plum Pudding. Sago & Tapiocca Pudding. I think some kind of Tart. Dessert, Nuts, Almonds, Raisins. Figs, [?] biscuits.

After dinner disported on deck till tea time.

All sails have been set the whole day. Stunsails likewise. We are before the wind. After Tea smoked a pipe.

9^{H}. Night prayers.

9^{H}.30^{M}. Punch. Whisky. Brandy & Rum.

Said Rosary on deck with Father Newman.

I added a good bit to my letter today as it is hoped that we may meet a homeward bound ship one of these days. Smoked in the night till 11^{H}.20^{M} PM. Rest.ships course S.W. by W.

Monday 12th

Rose at 7^{H}.50^{M}. M Prayers. The quantity of water we have been receiving this week past is very small indeed. Scarcely suffice.

9^{H}. On deck. All sails set wind N.E by N. Course S.W. by W.

Sail rate 7½ knots. Saw two sculls of flying fish to day pretty looking things they are about the size of a large sardine.[189] Said M & L on deck.

Breakfast.9^{H}.30^{M} Fare: Mutton Chops. Broiled Ham & eggs. Sliced Potatoes. Cold Tongue. Curry I think. Rice. Bread stale and black. Ship biscuit. Tea & c.

Saw some kind of Petrels about the ship.

11^{H}. Studying.

12^{H}. On Deck.

1^{H}. Study.

2^{H}. Read my trans to the Archbishop also read 3 chaps of Ecclues.[190]

3^{H}.40^{M}. Went on deck and found the course of Vessel changed to S. by W. ½ W.

12^{H}. Lat 17.48, Long 22 & a few miles.

---

188. Athy does not elaborate on the 'misfortune'.

189. 'Sculls'. Obscure dialect, English variation of 'school'.

190. '3 chapters of Ecclesiasticus'. An Old Testament book in the Bible.

Saw lots of flying fish today they are very curious looking things and very pretty. They fly very fast. They are started by the Vessel just fly about 10 or 15 yards and then light in the water again. Their wings are white something like gauze.

$4^{H}.30^{M}$. Dinner. Fare: Roast Leg Mutton. Boiled Turkey. boiled Fowl. [?]. Veal. Bacon & Curry. Rice. Puddings, Rice & Sago or Tapiocca Tarts. Vegetables, Potatoes. Turnips. Carrotts. Cabbage. Ale & Porter. Wines. Port & Sherry. No Dessert.

After dinner went on deck. Dr Gregory, who by the bye is the life and soul of whole party, got up a lark which gave us all plenty of exercise. He had an india rubber ball, hollow, this he used to fill with water, it had a very small hole through which when squeezed, it discharged the water in a jet and wet you all. He went about the deck squirting this at every one. There was such running about to get out of the way.

$7^{H}.30^{M}$. Tea. Bread & biscuits. Sliced Tongue. Yarmouth Bl. Porter. Ale. Port & Sherry.

$11^{H}.30^{M}$. To bed. Rate of sailing about 7K.

Tuesday 13th

Rose at $6^{H}.30^{M}$. To day being the feast of all saints of the Order of St B Mass was celebrated by the Archbishop at about $7^{H}.30^{M}$.[191]

M. Prayers and M. & L. before Mass. This morning a flying fish was caught (by one of) the sailors, it flew on the ship and was picked up.[192] In appearance it is very like a mullet and about the size of moderately sized herring. There are lots of flying fish about the ship today. Went on deck at $8^{H}.20^{M}$. Very fine, a nice breeze, a strong current against us.

Last night we passed some of the Cape De Verd Islands and we shall pass others of them to day but we shall not go near enough even to sight them.[193] Good bye now to the hope of sending letters by a homeward bound ship - The Capts intention at first was to pass through the Islands where we might have fallen in with some ship

191. 'St B' refers to St Benedict.
192. 'by one of'. These words written by Athy, then crossed out but are necessary to make sense of the sentence.
193. Cape De Verd Islands: Nowdays spelt 'Cape de Verde Islands'.

homeward bound. He afterwards altered his mind as he found the breeze so good so we ran between the Islands and the main land of Africa. All sails set this morning stunsails and all. Wind [*blank*]. Course S.E. by W.

Bkfst at $9^{H}.30^{M}$. Fare: Chops. Liver & bacon. Mashed ling. Curry. Boiled Potatoes. Rice. Stirabout. Bread & Biscuit. Tea. Butter.

10^{H}. On deck gaffing till near 11^{H}.[194] In cabin writing this journal. I shall now go to study my latin. Saw some queer kind of birds flying about the ship. Also some Petrels.

12^{H}. Weather very hot. I do not find my pilot trousers as yet too hot I wear them every day. I fancy that they seem to keep out the heat of the sun. And as on board ship one does not create much heat by exercise they have little to keep in. 12^{H} Lat [*blank*] Long [*blank*].

Lunch. I did not go so I do not know what was served. In honour of the feast did not read my exercise to day. Lots of dolphins playing under the bow to day. The sea is alive with flying fish. I shall go on deck and read 'The War'.

$3^{H}.0^{M}$. Went to cabin of His Grace to say office for the dead as tomorrow is All Souls of the order.

$4^{H}.30^{M}$. Dinner. After which we had larking on the deck some syringes having been procured we squirted water at each other; I had the sleeve of my coat torn at the commencement so I gave up. It was got up by Dr Gregory to give us exercise and employment.

Wednesday 14th

$6^{H}.30^{M}$. Mass for the dead at about 7^{H}.30. Dr Gregory officiated.

$8^{H}.15^{M}$. On deck. All sails set. Weather very fine but very hot. Course S. Lat 12.20. Long [*blank*].

$9^{H}.30^{M}$. Bkfst. Mutton chops. Eggs and bacon. Stirabout. Curry. Rice. Mashed Ling. Boiled Potatoes. Bread & butter. Biscuits. Tea.

After bkfst on deck till 11^{H}. Prepare exercise. Some of the rest playing draughts and chess. Others reading.

12^{H}.30. Lunch.

194. 'gaffing'. Means idle talk, prattling.

2^{H}. Read exercise to the Archbish and also some spiritual books till 3^{H}.15 when I joined the Archbishop and the Benedictines in reciting the Divine office.[195]

$4^{H}.30^{M}$. Dinner: Leg mutton boiled. Meat Pie. Boiled Ducks. Fowl. Ham. Curry. Some stews. Pudding: Sago & Tarts. Wines. Port & Sherry.

After dinner we played hunt the Monkey. It is played in this manner. One fellow, the Monkey, is tied by the waist with a rope strung from one of the ladders. All the rest have their pocket handkerchiefs knotted with which they lay on the monkey soundly but as soon as he touches anyone either with handkerchief or foot, he must become monkey himself in his place. This afforded great fun and exercise.

$6^{H}.20^{M}$. Said Office for the Dead with His Grace, that is the members of the Order and myself. The Office is for the Defunct relatives and benefactors of the Order.

$7^{H}.30^{M}$. Tea as usual Preserves, biscuits, bread & butter.

Thursday 15

Rose at $8^{H}.30^{M}$.

9^{H} 30^{M}. Bkfst, Fare: Pork Chops. Cold ham sliced. Some sort of mince baked. The rest as usual.

Day very fine and excessively hot. All sails set. Wind easterly. Course due South.

On deck till 11^{H}.30. Study and writing these notes.

12^{H}. Lunch. Lat 10.12 Long [*blank*].

$1^{H}.45^{M}$. Read to the Archbishop.

3.15. Said Office.

$4^{H}.30^{M}$. Dinner. As I was too lazy in this very hot weather to write these notes on the day itself, I have forgotten the bill of Fare. After dinner played at a romping game called hunt the Monkey. To bed at 1^{H}.15. We had singing [*at*[Punch time I sang "Come Landlord fill us a flowing bowl".

195. The members of the Benedictine Order on board the *Phoenix* were Archbishop Polding, Dr Gregory, Anselm Curtis and Mellitus Corish, as well as the Benedictine nuns.

Friday 16th

Rose at $9^{H}.0^{M}$.

Breakfast 9.30. Fare: Boiled Salt Ling. Pickled Salmon. Potatoes. Some sliced ham & c.

10^{H} to $11^{H}.30$. On deck lolling about and perspiring profusely, the fact is that for some days I have been in an uninterrupted state of perspiration. I wear my light Alpaca Coat, but Pilot trousers. I do not know how I shall ever get through these fearful tropics.

Wrote exercise for the Abp.

2^{H}. Went to His Grace to read it.

3.15. Office.

4.30. Dinner. Fare: Soup Vermicelli. Mutton pie. Stewed Ducks. Fowl boiled. Bacon. Pickled Salmon. Mashed Ling. Puddings. Rice & Maccaroon Tarts. Wines. Port.[196] Sherry. Claret.

After dinner Dr Gregory got up some sport for the steerage passengers. There was a pail full of water into which were thrown a sixpence and some apples which they were to take out with their mouths'. The Trinity College fellow whose name is Hopkins took out the first. He is a much better fellow than we at first thought.

After this we had a short game amongst ourselves called French blindmans buff. This finished, Dr Gregory with an admirable spirit of fun got up a dance on deck amongst the steerage passengers. He had some trouble in setting it going, as they were rather bashful at first. A fiddler was procured who played for them and some of the Paddies footed it well. Hopkins danced a Polka with, I do not know who, but she was the looking girl of the lot, Irish too. Between playing & dancing the sport was kept up till about 9^{H} or 10^{H} [?] We sang some jolly songs in the Cuddy at Punch time.[197] Success to the sensible Benedictines. There is no Pecksniffian cant about them.

Lat 7.41.

Saturday 17

Rose at $7^{H}.0^{M}$. Morning very fine breeze light from the E.

9^{H}. Bkfst. Chops, Liver & bacon. Cold tongue. Curry. Rice & c.

---

196. 'maccaroon' is as written. Now spelt 'macaroon'.

197. A 'Cuddy' is a small cabin formerly a saloon under the poop deck; also the gallery or pantry of a small vessel.

$10^{H}.0^{M}$. On deck. O! this tropical weather is enough to kill one, here I am in my cabin writing this and perspiring like an ox. I have been so for the last three or four days. When it will stop I do not know but I fancy that I shall be reduced in size considerably. In the last two nights I could not attempt to sleep in my berth so very hot has the weather become.[198] I took my pillow and rug and lay myself down on the benches in the saloon and slept there with my head level with the ventilator. I shall do the same as long as the hot weather continues.

Reading till 12. Lunch did not [?]. No lessons. Study. Confessions. Wind is light. Lots of petrels have been about ship.

Weather excessively sultry, ship hardly making any way. I shall sleep tonight in the Cuddy. I cannot stand these small Cabins in such very hot weather. I am writing this on Tuesday 20 Nov. The weather was so hot that one can scarcely do anything. I forget the bill of Fare.

Sunday 18

Rose a little after 6^{H}.

Mass 7.45. Went to Holy Communion.

Breakfast at 9.30. I must be off for the present as I am wanted on deck for some humbugging game.

Tuesday Nov 20[199]

We had no game after all; but as it got late and rather dark I did not resume this till next morning.

Some of us had the happiness of approaching the Most Holy today. O how consoling it is here alone I am on the great deep, though I am with as pleasant a party as could be by possibility be got together yet the fact of having parted for ever with one's own dearest ones, causes a blank, a feeling of hopeless loneliness, which no created beings can fill up or dispel; it is then that Most Holy Eucharist more than supplies for the pain of what would otherwise be so dismal a separation; it is

198. 'two nights'. This could be 'five nights', hard to decipher.

199. Athy entered Tuesday Nov 20 ahead of Monday 19 in his Journal. He then made another entry for Tuesday 20 following the Monday entry. He also entered Thursday 22 ahead of Wednesday 21 entry, when the *Phoenix* crossed the equator. I have put Thursday's entry in the correct position.

consoling I say to look forward to the time when I shall be permitted to receive. Mass over we walk about say our prayers, & make our thanksgivings for about 1½ hours.

Then Breakfast. Fare: Broiled Ham & Eggs the remainder pretty much the same as last Sunday.

11^{H}. After Bkfst we saunter about, some reading others meditating till $12^{H}.30^{M}$. We had likewise afternoon prayers read by Dr Gregory. The Jesus Psalter it was, at least a part of it and a beautiful prayer it is. What a pity that in England in the new books, I mean the very recent ones, it is not inserted.

Monday 19

Rose at $8^{H}.30^{M}$. All sails set weather fair.

Lat [*blank*] Long [*blank*]. Bkfst as usual and the same of the other meals. I say the Divine Office now regularly with the Archbishop & Benedictines.

I forgot to mention that for some time back we have much longer days full light now at 5^{H}. Weather excessively hot. Every one perspiring profusely.

Tuesday 20

Rose at $7^{H}.0^{M}$. Slept last night on the form in the Cuddy. Meals as usual. Nothing particular to day. We expect to cross the Line tomorrow. I hear that the sailors will not be permitted to play any tricks. Sighted a brig, homeward bound.

Crossed the Line

Wednesday 21st

It was hoped that we should have been able to have Mass today, but we were disappointed as the ship rolled too much.

It is the feast of the 'Presentation'. Rose at $6^{H}.25^{M}$. Weather fine a side wind rather ahead of us. Course S.W. by W. Lat [*blank*] Long [*blank*].

Bkfst $9^{H}.30^{M}$. Minces. Hash. Broiled Ham. Cold Ham. Rice. Stirabout & c Potatoes.

At about $11^{H}.30^{M}$ we Crossed The Line. We are now in the South Atlantic Ocean. Long [*blank*].

12^{H}. Lunch. After lunch spent some time reading & c.

3.15. Office Divine with His Grace and the Benedictines.

Thursday 22

Rose at $8^{H}.30^{M}$. Rosary.

Bkfst 9.30. Fare: Curry. Broiled Ham. Cold sliced Ham. Red Herrings. Rice. Stirabout. Tea. Bread & Butter.

10. On deck very fine day nice breeze temperature moderate sea rolling. Course S. W. by S.

Friday 23th

I have let this journal get into arrears. I am now trying to write it up in a sort of a way, I am writing in my cabin on Tuesday 27 Nov so excuses must be made as I forget most of what happened, indeed nothing of consequence happens now we see nothing but sea & sky not even a ship is to be seen breaking the monotony of the waves.

I see that the folks on board generally keep the abstinence on Friday, those of our party. There is no obligation of any kind sensibly.

Lat 5.3.

I have leave from His Grace to take malt liquor at dinner, the water has become so very nasty. For dinner we had pickled Psalm and mashed ling. Roast Pork, besides Curry & Mashes & Fowl.[200]

Saturday 24th

Very fair weather. Latitude 8.22.

No lessons to day it being confession day.

Sunday 25

Mass at 7.30. His Grace celebrated.

200. He has written 'Psalm' but possibly he intended to write 'salmon'.

A sword fish and shark seen. Lat 11.32.

This sea voyage is fearfully monotonous, the same six and fourpence every day.

Bkfst 9^{H}.30^{M} afterwards lounging about till 11^{H}.0^{M} then prayers in English.

12^{H}. Lunch.

3^{H}. I went with the Benedictines to His Grace's cabin to say Matins and Lauds which lasted till about 4^{H} then went on deck till 4^{H}.30^{M}. Dinner. The dinners as you have seen by the bills of Fare which I have given are pretty good.

7^{H}.30^{M}. Tea.

9.30. Punch. After which I generally go on deck to have a quiet pipe.

11^{H}.30^{M}. Bed.

Monday 26

Rose at 7^{H}.30^{M}.

8^{H}. I went to say the little hours with His Grace.

Lat [*left blank*].

Tuesday 27

Mass at 7.30. Father Keatinge celebrated.

Weather excessively fine. I was not very well today, I have been sick last night.

Lat [*blank*].

Wednesday 28

Rose at 7^{H}.15^{M}. Prime & Little Hours with His Grace.

Bkfst 9^{H}.30. Fare: Broiled bones. Fowl. Pork Chops. Corn Round Beef, Cold. Curry. Rice etc. Potatoes. Jam.

Weather very fine. Very slight breeze so much so that some of the sailors took a dip this morning in the sea, a rope being fastened round their waists.

Saw some pilot fish about the ship.

Wind [*blank*].

Course [*blank*] Lat [*blank*].

Well I have put off finishing this till today or rather tonight Thursday 29th but it matters little as nothing worth recording has occurred and as I have given so many of the bills of fare there is not much to interest on that subject now so I need not rack my brain to remember what we had for dinner.

Were becalmed nearly all day. Went to bed at 11.30. Still a dead calm.

Thursday 29th

Rose at about 7H.30M.

8H. Little Hours with His Grace, whom may God bless and preserve for his exceeding kindness and the trouble he takes with me, he is really a father to me and I thank God for having so disposed things to enable me to be with him.

Went on deck at about 9H.0M. Slight breeze I do not remember from what quarter. Fine sunny day warm but not so smothering as yesterday.

9H.30M. Breakfast. Fare: Boiled Ling, (salt). Pork chops fresh. Cold round beef (corn). Stirabout. Rice, etc.

10H. Went on deck to smoke my dooder and wander about till 11H.30 when I went down to study.[201]

12H. Lunch of which I did not partake.

2H. Went to His Grace to read my translation from the Paradisus. English into Latin.

3H. Matins and Lauds with His Grace and the Benedictines.[202]

4H. On deck till 4H.30M.Dinner. Fare: Soup. Boiled Mutton. Roast Pork, both fresh as we killed a sheep and a Pig a day or two ago. Roast Goose. Boiled Fowl. Bacon. Curry. Vegetables, Potatoes and Preserved pease, which by the bye are no great shakes, one only eats them for the name of the thing. Wines. Port, Sherry. Champagne. Ale & Porter.

Just before dinner we sighted an outward bound Ship, distant about 8 or 10 miles the first we have seen for a long time. She stood

201. A 'dooder' is a type of smoker's pipe.
202. This how the word is spelt in the Journal, should be 'Matins'.

towards us and overhauled us as she at last came within five or six miles of us.

We did no[*t*] signalize her nor she us so I cannot give the particulars about her. She appeared to be bound, from the direction she was going, to Africa.

There is to be Mass tomorrow.

There was a slight cuffing match on deck today between the head steward and one of his underlings, but it did not come to much.

Lat [*blank*].

I shall soon go up and have a cigar and then to bed. 11^{H}.0^{M} P.M.

St Andrew[203]

Friday 30th

Rose at 6^{H}.30^{M}.

7^{H}.30. Mass. Archbishop celebrated. Office Little Hours with the Archbishop. Afterwards went on deck, nice Breeze. Wind N.N.E. Course by compass S.S.E. all sails set going at 8 knots.

9^{H}.30^{M}. Breakfast. Fare: Boiled Ling. Cod roe. Salt Herrings. Rice. Curry. Corn round beef. Stirabout.

I have lately found that all those who are able, abstain on the Fridays. Though there is no obligation to do so. It appears that of those who were in my immediate neighbourhood most were unable to abstain. I used not to abstain, but I shall commence now.

This morning we did not see the ship that followed us yesterday.

My thoughts this morning as they often do, turned homewards, I must begin to check this as it makes me melancholy. But yet it is not easy to do it here as among strangers one is thrown greatly on one's self.

But God be praised.

There has just this instant occurred an accident but happily no one was hurt. The sailors were tightening some of the rigging, something gave way and down came one of the blocks thundering through I believe a skylight into some cabin or other, I do not know which as I am writing this, and it has only just occurred what I have written are only the words of one passing by. I shall try to get particulars if I do succeed I shall record them.

203. 30 November is St Andrew's Feast Day.

I have just heard that the block did not fall from a height, a block which was fastened on the deck and with which they were tightening one of the stays, gave way and half of it went through a sky light. Had it hit any one it would certainly have brained him. I have now come down to read.

Only fancy what a miserable head I have. I am continually forgetting to lock my Portmanteau in which there are 91 sovereigns. I wonder whether my memory will ever improve.

How odd it seems to be in summer now, and tomorrow the 1stDec. I suppose that tomorrow or after the sun will be vertical. We are now in the hottest latitudes, but it is not very much too warm here owing to our being on the ocean, but were we in the same latitude on land the heat would be insupportable.

$11^{H}.30^{M}$. Study.

2^{H}. Repeating studies to His Grace.

3^{H}. Divine Office.

4^{H}. Walking on deck till $4^{H}.30^{M}$ when we went to dinner. Fare: Pea Soup. Roast Pork. Some kind of meat Pie. Fowl of some kind or other. Pickled Salmon off which the abstainers dined. Sweets. Rice Puddings. Gooseberry and Plum (preserved) Tarts. Cheese every day. Wines. Port & Sherry.

As yet I have only seen one sun set which at all approached the sun sets of dear old Renville. We have not seen the Southern Cross the constellation does not rise till 2^{H} or 3^{H} in the morning however I hope that in a few days more we shall see it. I manage to get some comfortable whiffs of the pipe every day. In the evening there are one or two who join me. Lat [*blank*].

This journal is a rambling affair as I do not write it regularly, all by fits and starts. So you must excuse it. I am afraid it will not make you much wiser. I have now to scrape up the latitudes for this last week, I hope some one may be charitable enough to give them to me. How I wish that dear F Lockhart was with us. I wonder whether I shall ever see him again.[204] I wish that "The End of the World" would take it into his head to send him out. I am selfish enough for that, though I know how you would all howl.

It is near prayer time so I must shut up just 9^{H} somewhere about 11^{H} with you I suppose.

---

204. Father Lockhart: See p 36 of Athy biography for more information.

December

Saturday 1st

Rose $7^{H}.40^{M}$. Little Hours at 8^{H}.

Afterwards went on deck. All sails set. Rattling fair breeze.

9^{H}. Spoke a Ship, Bark, the *Aurora* from Callao. She did not reply to our question as to where she was bound, reported her latitude as [*blank*]. The Mate told me that he supposed she was homeward bound either to Falmouth or Queenstown.[205] Were not sufficiently near to send letters on board.

Bkfst at $9^{H}.30^{M}$. Fare: Pork Chops (Fresh). Some sort of mess of meat, potatoes, onions which was very good. Curry. Cold round beef (corn). Stirabout, etc.

Went on deck and smoked a cigar.

I shall read a little now and then prepare for confession. It is well that it is a pecksniff day as I am rather dull and that will cheer me up.

One of these days I must make a journey to the depths below to see about my box No 2 and to examine whether the damp is doing any injury. The other day some of the passengers went down and found that their things had got mildewed.

Pecksniff going on till dinner time.

4.30. Dinner. Fare: Soup. Veal pie. Roast Pork. Boiled Fowl. Curry. Bacon. Sweets. Rice Pudding. Green gage & Gooseberry, I believe, tarts. Cheese. Wines. Port. Sherry. Malt, Ale, Beer, & Porter every day. Afternoon wet and a bit of a swell.

Our Course S.S.E. Wind about N.E. Rate from 8 to 10 knots per hour.

Smoking after dinner.

7.30. Tea. Smoking.

9^{H}. Novena for the Immaculate Conception & Night Prayers.

9.30. Grog time, afterwards Smoking, this latter affair only enjoyed by a select few.

---

205. Cork. This locality, which had several Irish-language names, was first called Cove ('The Cove of Cork') in 1750. The name was changed to Queenstown on 2 August 1849 to commemorate a visit by Queen Victoria (1819-1901). This remained the town's name until 1922 when it was renamed Cobh with the foundation of the Irish Free State. Cobh is a gaelicization of the English name Cove and has no meaning in the Irish language See http://www.cork-guide.ie/cobh.htm http://www.vssj.jp/journal/7/kelly.pdf Accessed 22 September 2015.

$10^{H}.30^{M}$. Rest. Rain has now stopped.
Latitude of today [*blank*].

Sunday 2

1st Advent.[206]

Rose at $6^{H}.10^{M}$ and was shouting all the morning for water to wash with, of which by the bye the quantity dealt out is very small indeed. I do not think that you have a pint, certainly not more and this is supposed to do you for the whole day, and between two persons. The consequence is that you have not wherewith to wash hands before dinner. Well I got the allowance of water at about $6^{H}.45^{M}$.

$7^{H}.30^{M}$. Mass.

A great number went to Holy Communion this morning among whom were several of the steerage folks from St Patrick's land.

If it were not for Mass and Holy Communion I think that I should die of the blues. O how tiresome this sea voyage is, nothing to be seen but Ocean and sky day after day. This Capt. does not like going within viewing distance of any land.

Well from Mass till $9^{H}.30^{M}$ Pecksniff going on. 9^{H}. Saw a vessel a head of us. We had some of our sails reefed up this morning and from stress of weather as the breeze was veery.

But it was so much aft that the mainsails kept the wind from the others before them so they had to be reefed up.

$9^{H}.30^{M}$. Breakfast. Fare: Pork Chops. Mashed Meat & Potatoes. Cold round beef. Curry & c.

10^{H} to 11^{H}. On deck getting fresh air.

11^{H}. Prayers in English read by F. Keatinge.

12.30. Lunch.

1^{H} to $2^{H}.30^{M}$. Sauntering about the deck.

2.30. I went to read Scripture and Paradisus to His Grace.

3^{H}. Office.

$4^{H}.30^{M}$. Dinner. Meat Pie. (Natural. Veal). Veal (pickled) pudding. Roast Fowl. Boiled Salt Pork, Roast Pork (Fresh), Curry. Potatoes which by the bye are not the best. Preserved Peas, no great things. Malt, Ale & Porter. Wines. Port. Sherry. Champagne. The latter wine

206. First Sunday of Advent.

is given but sparingly only two bottles to about four & twenty people. Sweets: Plum pudding. Tapioca pudding. Tarts.

After dinner we did not [*do*] much. I had my smoke both after dinner and tea. Rest 11^{H}.30^{M}.

Monday 3

St F Xavier.[207] Rose at 6^{H}.10^{M}. Mass at 7.30. I received the Holy Communion. Prayers [*of*] thanksgiving and Office till 9^{H}.30^{M}.

Bkfst Fare: boiled bones. Mutton chops. Cold Corn round beef. Cold sliced Pork (salt) & c.

10^{H} to 12^{H}. I examined the dirty clothes in my carpet bag and found all safe.

12^{H}. Lunch I adjourned to my cabin to write this. I must tell you that, Hopkins that fellow I have already mentioned two or three times comes from near Athboy Co Meath, he is a pretty good sort of a fellow.

O this sea voyage is very monotonous, it is almost enough to kill one with the blues. The day is very fine but the breeze very light. I shall be so glad when we land.

Tuesday 4th

7^{H}.15^{M}. Office and prayers as usual. Breakfast as usual.

10^{H}. Went on deck all sails set breeze very light about then fell a calm.

There was a shark bait put out, but I am sorry to say without any fortunate results.

People talked a great deal of the number of sharks in the oceans, but really we have not had ocular demonstration of the fact and were they in such numbers we must have seen some at least as in fine weather, nay in all weathers I believe that they are close to the surface and in calm warm weather then show above water. Now and again you hear a fellow hallowing out there is a shark, look and pointing somewhere with his finger but somehow or other I have never been so fortunate as to see it though looking in the direction indicated.

207. 3 December is the Feast Day of St Francis Xavier.

When you come to enquire, only the fin was visible and that must have been at least 100 yards away, if visible at all. The observations are always made by some of the passengers. As for me I never saw any of the sharks so that I really doubt, not their existence, but that they abound in these oceans in such numbers. Though were I to point out this it would be considered as rank heresy.

You have no idea what shifts are made in order to "amuse Grothman"[208]. Sometimes Hopkins brings down a rifle and pistol and blazes away at a bottle which has been thrown out for the purpose. Then again there are all sorts of folks playing at draughts and some few at chess. They have given up the rough games after dinner, and really I am very glad of it as they destroyed ones clothes. I know I have some shirts which I fear are utterly ruined by the games. I had to put them up wet with perspiration and the tobacco in the bag stained them. I sent them to undergo a preliminary washing the other day, for really they are so discoloured that I was ashamed to do with them as the others did with theirs, to hang them out to air.

12^{H}. Lunch as usual.

I forgot to mention an equiviacto which will make Randal laugh and which occurs every morning at 8^{H}.0. You hear all of a sudden a fellow at the head of the cabin stairs shouting out:

"Are you ready Sir?"

"All Ready!"

Then after a second or two you hear the Captain shout "Stop" which is re-echoed by the chap at the head of the stairs.

Then you hear the Skipper shout something like this – "24 – 2 – 10", which is re-echoed by the fellow at the head of the stairs and duly recorded by the Mate in the Skipper's cabin. This goes on for about five minutes, the numbers though are different every time. I do not know of what nature, but the numbers are the results of observations taken by the Skipper with the quadrant.

At 12^{H} you know he takes the Longitude and Latitude.

They say that the Southern Cross is visible now. I have not seen it as yet. The stars here are wonderfully clear and bright I wish that Bessy could see them.[209] She would be enchanted. Orion here is a

208. This is a guess at the word. It has been suggested that 'Grothman' could be a character in a novel or play that has become a saying.

209. Athy had a sister called Elizabeth born c1819.

magnificent constellation, it is turned topsy turvy the sword being on top instead of below thus -

[*here he drew the lie of the constellation*]

We used to have singing in the evening and my song 'Come Landlord' took amazingly. I had to sing the verse "Punch is the surest remedy for evil" three or four times. Likewise Father Gills' verse "He that can drink and will not drink but spare it". Latterly we have not had any songs.

Made a fast of today without abstinence as there was nothing but meat for dinner.

Wednesday 5th

Rose at 7H.10M. Morning employed as normal. Fast Day. Good breakfast but did not partake of it. Fellows of such iron constitutions as I can easily keep the fasts.

I forgot yesterday to mention that a ship was sighted from aloft though not from the deck.

We are on the lookout for the Albatross and a bird called Cape Pigeon. As yet we have not seen them. There were some petrels about yesterday and a "green devil" also flying about of the size of Whimbrel and somewhat like a hawk.[210]

This morning there is a nice breeze. I suppose that we are going at about seven knots at least now.

11H. All sails are set. Course S.S.E. by compass [*blank*] Wind [*blank*] E. Lat 27.5. Long 16.

11H.55M. Studies. I have just come off deck. I shall now read and study and show the Archbishop the results, till about 2H.50M. I am determined not to neglect to get the latitude and longitude to day.

To day the atmosphere is very pleasant not a bit too hot. Only fancy they tell me that it is daylight now at 4H.0M. I shall, this evening enter the time of sunset, then again the time when darkness falls. Darkness fell at about 7H.15M. I did not see the sunset. I fancy that it was no great thing.

---

210. A 'Whimbrel' is a migratory bird of the curlew family and grows to about 40 to 45 centimetres.

Fasted to day could not abstain there being nothing for dinner but meat. Fare: Soup. Boiled leg Mutton. Roast do.[211] Preserved Meat pie. Boiled Fowl. Boiled Pork. Irish stew. Sweets: Tapiocca Puddings. Tarts. Gooseberry and Plum (preserved). Wines. Port & Sherry. Malt ale. Porter. Did nothing but saunter about after dinner. One of our Party is unwell, some rheumatic attack.

I shall go now and smoke a weed. It being Punch time, $9^{H}.30^{M}$PM. Bed $11^{H}.10^{M}$.

Thursday 6th

$7^{H}.0^{M}$. Pecksniff as usual.

9.30. Breakfast. Fare: Hash. Dry Hash, this is more properly a mash of meat and potatoes, in a large pie dish. Cold salt pork sliced. Stirabout. The batter is not what [?] would call good. After Breakfast went on deck. Weather very fine. All sails set. Wind N.E. by E. Course S.S.E. Those who used to get the sailors to spout sea water on them out of the fire engine have been obliged to give it up as they have all been unwell. They used to go up on deck at 6^{H}, when the decks were being washed, and used to get the sailors to play their engine on them the decks being washed by the engine. I think that the spouting and rough after dinner games have knocked them up.

There is an Australian, passenger, in second cabin he is a very plain man, but a most worthy man, a convert whom they say is worth over £20,000. To look at him you would not value him at as many shillings.

11.10. I came down to cabin to write this and then to study. I shall enter the Lat at 12^{H}. The weather is still warm though not so oppressive as it was a fortnight ago.

My mate keeps continually running in and out of the cabin. And now he has taken to write music and is at this moment humming Do re mi fa so & c which is very moidering.[212] What a nuisance people become when they fancy they can sing somewhat better than others.

Latitude 28.38S & Longitude 15 W.

12. Lunch. I study at this hour till about 2^{H} when I go to read my exercises to His Grace.

3^{H}. Office.

---

211. 'do' is Latin abbreviation for 'ditto'.

212. 'Moidering' (origin uncertain), to distract, perplex, bother, worry.

$4^{H}.30^{M}$. Dinner. Fare: Soup. Boiled Corn Beef. Preserved Veal Pie, this today was detestable the meat having a very rank taste. Roast Fowl & Boiled salt Pork in lieu of Bacon. Something Roast at the other end of table Mutton I rather think. Irish Stew. Sweets. Tapiocca Puddings. Plum Tarts. Cheese & c. Wine. Champagne, a Bottle. Port & Sherry, Ale & Porter.

After dinner on deck, some playing draughts, others chess. Also walking about or sitting down chatting.

To day just before dinner we saw a bird about the size of a middle size hen, apparently flying in our wake. Called a Cape Hen a queer looking devil. Some of the Cabin passengers fired at it but missed it, at which I was very glad for had it been shot they could never have got it and I see no sense in shooting a thing merely for the sake of killing it. Tea. Punch as usual. Retire at 11.20.

Friday 7th

Rose $7^{H}.30$. Pecksniff as usual.

Morning pretty fine and showers of rain.

Wind has changed at last and our side of the vessel is the lea side for the first time since we left Liverpool.[213] Ship is only going 5½ knots per hour as we lie so close to wind. Course E by S. Wind S.E. by E. Latitude [*blank*] Longitude [*blank*]. Breeze is pretty fresh though not quite favourable.

It is extraordinary we have not seen either the Albatross or Cape Pigeons as yet. Neither have we seen the Southern Cross.

It is just Lunch time so I must shut up for the present and betake myself to my translation from Paradisus and Breviary.

Breeze very fresh. Ship lying well over to the larboard so much so as to make it difficult rather to pace the deck.[214] Temperature rather cool. We are just going to dinner so I shall shut up.

It is well I mended my box yesterday. The one you dearest Ma bought for me. The hinges started and the clasp likewise when we were somewhere about the bay of Biscay and I let it remain open till yesterday.

---

213. Correct spelling of the 'lea' side would be 'lee' side.
214. 'Larboard' is the left hand side of the ship, from a passenger's viewpoint as they face the bow.

I think that we shall have a rough night of it people will be sick again.

$4^{H}.30^{M}$. Dinner. Fare: Roast Mutton. Preserved Salmon. Soup, pea. Bacon and liver. Sweets: Rice Pudding. Plum & gooseberry Tarts. Cheese. Wines. Port. Sherry. Porter & Ale.

After dinner to day could not go on deck till later there being heavy rain. We had to reef many of the sails as it blew very heavy.

In the evening I went on deck as the rain cleared off and smoked my pipe or rather cigar.

11^{H}. Rest.

Saturday 8

Feast of the Immaculate Conception.

6^{H} AM Rose.

$7^{H}.40^{M}$. Mass. Several of us went to Holy Communion to day. We were very much afraid yester-evening that the weather would be too rough to permit of the celebration of Mass and even this morning up to nearly $7^{H}.30^{M}$ it was doubtful. But our Blessed Lady took pity on us poor exiles and stilled the sea somewhat, so to our great comfort The Holy Sacrifice was celebrated by His Grace.

My dearest Mother and Bessy I thought of you, as well as of dearest Cat and Randal this morning, and I know that, probably, a couple of hours before you both were going to communion and thinking of me so that though separated in space, we are in reality closely united.[215] The Most Holy Body of Our Lord unites us, absent from each other according to the flesh, with a band of exquisite charity. And I reason

215. Athy's youngest sister, Catherine born c1829. His mother, Bridget Athy, his sisters Elizabeth and Catherine were all living in London at the time Athy was sailing to Sydney – he mentions that in his Journal entry of Christmas Day. (Bessy is a diminutive of Elizabeth, Cat is a shortened form of Catherine). At the end of 1856, Martha Lockhart, (the mother of Father Lockhart, also named in this Journal) accompanied by Catherine Athy, moved from Greenwich to Kingsland, London so the older woman could be near her son. Nicholas Schofield, the author of a biography on Father William Lockhart writes that "a house on Culford Road was rented by Mrs Lockhart and Miss Athy, who had also belonged to the Sisters of Charity of the Precious Blood at Greenwich. She was later joined by her sister and mother." Just how long they had been in England is unknown.

that you were likewise praying for me, that on this my birthday the grace of being born to a new life would be vouchsafed to me. I am very sure that the prayers of that little Angel Cat were offered also for me so that I am well provided with prayers.[216] And what is of more value than all, the prayers of dear F Lockhart in his Mass. It is a rare mercy from Almighty God to have so placed me that numberless petitions from good and holy souls are continually ascending to His throne for one, who has been immersed in the lowest depths of iniquity. Praise be to His Holy Name.

Pecksniff till $9^{H}.30^{M}$.

Breakfast: A mash of meat & Potatoes. Mutton Chops. Hot Hash of Mutton I believe. Yarmouth bloaters to which I paid my devoirs.[217] Tea etc.

Went on deck. Breeze light and a heavy swell on. Wind S.E. by E. Course, S. by E.

His Grace has given a holiday today to us who were under his tuition. This is a glorious day' ratione festi'.[218]

Today I endeavoured to read Russell on the war but somehow or other I felt so very sleepy that I did not make much way.

12. Lunch.

3^{H}. Office. As there was a pretty heavy swell on at this hour, sitting on stools in the Archbishop's cabin was rather a job so much so that at one time I lost my equilibrium during one of the Psalms and was nearly pitched on top of my neighbour. This upset my gravity for some time.

4^{H} 0^{M}. Went on deck and saw an Albatross he did not appear to be of such an enormous size, about twice as large as one of the Black backed Gulls you see over the west coast of Ireland. There were six Cape Hens following us all day.[219] One or two of them came quite close to the ship so that I could see what they were like. I forget whether I described them before or not. I know that I mentioned them. Well for fear of omission here goes. They are about as large as a large Curlew. Of a very dark brown. A good deal of white about the

216. Athy was born 8 December 1818.
217. 'Devoirs' means to pay one's duty; and act of civility or respect.
218. 'ratione festi' is Latin for 'because of the feast'.
219. Here Athy, reaching the end of the page and missed two pages. He then went back near the end of today's entry and continued to write in the overlooked pages.

head, the bill apparently that of a gull. In fact they are neither more nor less than the kind of sea gull common to these Latitudes. The Albatross has very long and pointed wings. Grey over the wings and back. Breast and butt of tail very white. Some fellows were firing at these poor Cape Hens and I am sorry to say wounded some of them. I see no sense in firing at a bird when you know to a certainty that you cannot get them when shot. I think that it is deliberate cruelty.

$4^{H}.30^{M}$. Dinner. Fare: Soup. Mutton boiled & Roast. Fowl. Pickled Pork. Hash of some kind. Sheep's head boiled. A detestable pie made of preserved veal of which I partook but with which I could not get through. I met a very suspicious looking kind of fat which by the bye I started, it did not taste very bad but it looked nasty. Sweets: Rice Puddings. Tarts, Greengages. Port. Sherry. Porter. Ale.

Ship pitching a good deal so much so as to send bottles and plates sliding about the table if you were not on the lookout for such like squalls.

Tea at $7^{H}.0^{M}$. Afterwards at $9^{H}.30^{M}$ I went to smoke.

Sun set today at $7^{H}.0^{M}$ PM.

11^{H}. Bed.

Thermometer & Barometer were fixed up to day.

Sunday 9th

$6^{H}.10^{M}$. Rise.

There is such a swell on today we cannot have Mass which is such privation. I think that the high wind we got into on Friday evening must have been the outside circle of a cyclone for here to day the swell is much heavier than a wind such as we experienced on Friday could kick up. The centre of it must have been about here, for the swell is very heavy, and the Capt. said that there must have been a heavy gale to knock up such a sea. The weather is clear & sunny. Thermometer up to 70. Barometer 30.

$8^{H}.0^{M}$. Pecksniff with the Abp.

9.30. Breakfast. Fare: Pork Chops (Fresh). Broiled Ham. Dry Hash consists of meat & potatoes chopped together. Curry. Tea & c.

11^{H}. English prayers instead of Mass. I found it not easy to keep awake. Dr Gregory read them, he also read a long winded — fearing that you may not decipher the two last words they are "long winded" — sermon. I rather think it was one of Archers'.[220]

12H.40M. Lunch. Latitude 30.19 Long [blank].

As I was coming down to breakfast, just as I was entering the door of the house covering the stairs the ship gave a heave that brought my head in contact with the top of the door with a violence that knocked me down. But I was soon allright again.

One of our mates a Mr Murphy is laid up, in fact he has been laid up for some days. The combined effects I think of having the fire engine played on his person every morning, and playing at hunt the monkey and such like juvenile sports unsuitable I think to people of forty years. Besides, no time would do for these violent games but immediately after dinner ---.

I have just taken about an hour's snooze. I really felt so overpowered that I was obliged, in order to be fit for anything, to give way for a while.

It is now 11H.20M P.M. I have just come down to turn in, but first I must write up the rest of to day's journal.

Will commence with dinner. Fare: Soup, which was very good. Roast Pork fresh. Boiled Mutton. Corn Beef. Pickled Pork. Goose.

---

220. James Archer, Preacher. Archer (17th November, 1751 -22 August, 1832) was an English missionary priest, born in London.
While employed at a public house called *The Ship*, in Turn Stile, Lincoln's-Inn-Fields, where Catholics secretly assembled for Divine service, he attracted the favourable notice of Dr Richard Challoner, a major figure in English Catholicism, and was sent in 1769 to study at Douai College, France. Following ordination in 1780, he returned to England, to carry on the mission from the public house where he had formerly been employed. He was for many years Vicar-General of the London District and received the papal degree of Doctor of Divinity.
His published works are:
"*Sermons on Various Moral and Religious Subjects*" (London, 1787, 1788, 1816);
"*Second Series*" (London, 1801, 1822);
"*Third Series*" (London, 1827);
"*Sermons*" (London, 1789, 1794, 1817);
"*Sermons on Matrimonial Duties, etc.*" (London, 1804);
"*Letter to J. Milner, Vicar-Apostolic of the Midland District* (Being a Reply to a letter in which he accuses the author of immorality)" (London, 1810);
"*Sermon on Universal Benevolence — Some Reflections on Religious Persecution and the alleged proceedings at Nismes*" (2d ed., London, 1816).
See http://www.newadvent.org/cathen/01694d.htm Accessed 20 September 2015.

Curry. Vegetables, Carrotts & Potatoes. Sweets: a kind of Plum pudding. Tapiocca puddings. Some kind of tarts. Cheese. Wines. Port. Sherry. Champagne. Ale. Porter. Dessert, Nuts, Almonds, Raisins, Figs.

5.15. On deck lounging. There being a heavy sea now & the vessel pitching a good deal which she is doing likewise at this moment.

7^{H}.10. Tea, Bread, Biscuits, Butter, salt, Marmalade.

8.15. Pecksniff and Rosary with the Abp.

9^{H}. Night prayers. Afterwards I went on deck till $11^{H}.20^{M}$ and indulged in Pipe & Cigar. Now good night I am off to bed.

Monday 10

$7^{H}.0^{M}$. Rose. On deck. Swell had subsided.

Weather fine. Breeze middling. Course S.½E. by compass. Wind [*blank*].

8^{H}. Pecksniff.

$9^{H}.30^{M}$. Breakfast. Fare: Pork Chops, fresh. Broiled bones, (Fowl), Dry Hash. Curry. Cold corn beef, this was rather coarse, the Pork Chops were very good. Stirabout. One must eat here in self defence, otherwise one would be sick.

I shall be very glad when we land for I assure you that I have had quite enough of the sea, it would be pleasant enough, were we to pass near land anywhere, we then could see something but to be doomed for weeks to contemplate nothing but sky & water wherever you look this is horrible. The sea birds of which it was said we should see plenty, have turned out myths for comparatively speaking we have seen but few indeed. And as for sharks I have heard of a few of which I told you before but I have seen none.

We are now on the look out for the Albatross of which, they say, we must see plenty. Some of them measuring 16 feet from wing to wing.

You cannot imagine how difficult it is to write any sort of a journal in such a voyage, when you have but the same sort of news to record day after day. If this goes the round of the family it will disgrace me the matter being next to nil and the composition not being the best.

If I fail with the Benedictines I think that my head will be the cause. I now have become so stupid and my memory is so very bad. However I shall leave it all in the hands of the Archbishop who is taking immense pains with me. It will not be any fault of his if I do not get on.

Dr Gregory the other day popped his head into our cabin and said "Oh dear what an untidy pair you are", which I must say had some truth in it for everything was in confusion just then, indeed at best we are not very tidy, but on that day we appeared more so than usual as that lazy stewardess, a scotchwoman had not made our beds and it was about midday.

I do not think that I shall want chest No 2 at all on the voyage I have not half finished No 1. The sheets & c of which I have as yet only taken one, and that was to give to my comrade in lieu of one of his on which I spilt a bit of ink, not an uncommon occurrence with me. Seeing as how I have spattered many things with ink.

Ah! My dearest mother how I shall feel the want of you regarding my clothes and things, I fear I shall make a sad mess of it. I can hardly realize the fact of our entire separation. But may the Will of God be done. I shall not write more on this theme it makes me so very sad.

I must tell you that Hopkins whom I mentioned two or three times has proved to be a very nice fellow indeed. He is quite "hail fellow well met" with us all. He addresses all the Ecclesiastics as "Doctor". He calls me "Colonel" in return for which I have dubbed him "General" so you may hear these titles shouted out on the quarter deck with all the gravity imaginable. There is one man who we call "Governor" an Australian a good sort of fellow and rich. £20,000.

I shall go up on deck now to see what is up.

$12^{H}.0^{M}$. I have just come off deck, where I was meditating on many things, and you all composed a pretty fair share of my meditations. As I was looking over the taffrail which is the rail at the stern, two or three large birds, white and grey passed me at first sight they did not appear to be much larger than the black back gull I used to see in times past at dear Old Renville.[221] But what with not imaginative effect having heard so much said about the Albatross I concluded that these must be some of them and accordingly they grew in my eyes till I at last fancied them immense, though I persuaded myself of this with difficulty. So after satiating my eyes for about 20 minutes I went off to communicate the intelligence that there were two large Albatrosses following the ship.

---

221. 'tafrail': correct spelling is taffrail, the railing around the stern of a ship.

The first one to whom I pointed them out, who knew anything about them, was Father Keatinge, who immediately said they were not Albatrosses. I then appealed to the Capt. who at once dubbed them sea gulls. So after all they have turned out to be my old friends the grey backed gull I used to see at Renville. They pointed out a bird to us on Saturday as an Albatross which was identical in appearance to these. So I believe that it was a grey gull likewise, though they said not when I told them. I believe that it was.

The day is rather cloudy so much so that the Captain was unable to make his midday observations.

I must now shut up as I have to prepare my $2^{H}.0^{M}$ Lesson for the Archbishop.

They say that we shall stop some days at Melbourne, at which I am delighted as they say my dear friend Mr Parsons is stationed somewhere there so I shall have a chance of seeing him.[222]

At $12^{H}.0^{M}$ the Thermometer and Barometer in the Cuddy, the first was at 70, the latter a little above 30.

Unfortunate always, whilst in my cabin I heard one report two whales close to the ship, whereupon I sallied forth and when I got on deck they were not to be seen, $2^{H}.30^{M}$.

Lessons $3^{H}.10^{M}$.

Office at 4^{H}.

A ship in the offing we are not as yet up with her.

Dinner bell has just rung so I must away $4^{H}.30^{M}$.

Fare: Soup. Corn beef, boiled. Pork, fresh, Roast. One of those detestable Pies of which I did not partake. Boiled Fowl. I think Curry. Vegetables, Carrotts, Potatoes, Boiled and Roast.

Sweets: Rice Pudding. Tarts, Plum and greengages. Wines. Port & Sherry. Ale. Porter. Cheese. No dessert to day.

We are approaching the ship we sighted before dinner. She is outward bound. On the same course as ourselves. We shall come up to her about night fall. She appears to be very light in the water.

I shall go on deck now till tea time it is now $6^{H}.30$ in this latitude. I suppose about 8^{H} with you.

$7^{H}.0^{M}$. Tea. After tea went up to see if we had overhauled the ship at all, found we had somewhat. It now appears that we shall not come up to her before 1^{H} or 2^{H} in the morning. Pecksniff & c as usual.

$11^{H}.20^{M}$. Bed.

222. See p 11 Athy Biography for more information.

Tuesday 11th

7H.30M. Pecksniff as usual.

There was a report this morning that some whales were to be seen, likewise an Albatross. But I have seen none of them so I can only record the report. I saw one of those large gulls. I strongly suspect it to be the bird they have dubbed as an Albatross.

9H.30M. Breakfast. Fare: Pork (Fresh) Chops. Dry Hash. Wet Hash. Cold sliced beef. Boiled Ling. Stirabout. Tea & c.

I afterwards went up to look out for some of these wonders! but as usual they are never to be seen when I am up. I'll bet anything that when I go up again I shall hear of something extraordinary. Perhaps the Sea Serpent will have been seen and plunged down to the depths just as I emerged from the Cuddy.

Course S. by E. Wind [*blank*].

12H.30. Lunch as usual. From 11.30 to 4H every day holidays excepted, Studies and Divine Office.

About 2H some porpoises seen about the ship of which I saw three swimming like mad, close to the surface, they appeared to be racing with the ship being close to her, and they shot ahead very fast and queer looking things they were. They did not roll at all but swam quite straight so you could see them well. We saw two or three Albatrosses to day they appeared to be somewhat larger than a goose. Some saw a shoal of porpoises but I did not.

4.20. Dinner. Fare: Soup. Roast Pork (Fresh). A pie, very indifferent. Bacon. Boiled Fowls. Curry. Vegetables, Potatoes, roast and Boiled. Sweets: Sago puddings. Tarts, gooseberry & Plum. Cheese. Port & Sherry. Ale & Porter.

7H. Tea. After Tea I went up to smoke a pipe. At about 11H Turned in. Saw the Southern Cross to night, it rather disappoints me. It is a cross turned upside down.

Rate of sailing at 10H when the log was heaved 5½ knots.

There will be Mass tomorrow.

Hopkins was blazing away to day with a rifle at the Albatross but without effect.

Wednesday 12

6H.30M. Rise. Pecksniff till 9. Mass celebrated by F Mellitus.

Two ships in sight in the offing. I saw this morning two sea-gulls old friends of mine, the common Tern, or Sea Swallow. I am sorry to say that one of them was fired at by some heartless fellow and wounded. He never could pick it up as they will not lower their boats for such trifles.

10^{H}. The ships sighted this morning in the offing now prove to be a brig and a ship.

I saw a whale at last, and bad luck to him he has made me appear like one who calls attention when he has seen nothing. I called peoples' attention to it just as it was going down, and as it did not appear again of course people said "there is a whale".

The weather is very fine, we have been for the last three days in the Indian Ocean.

Course S.S.E.

Breakfast. Fast Day. Pork (fresh) Chops. Ling boiled. Dry Hash. Mince. Potatoes. It is provoking that we could not partake of these Dainties.

On board ship people amuse themselves in different ways, some sitting talking, others smoking, among those I sometimes take my stand others playing chess & others draughts. There is on board a navvy, one of the lot sent by Peto & Company to Balaclava he is now on his way to Australia. He is a huge man looks an animal.[223]

12^{H}. This afternoon we have seen plenty of Albatrosses and four or five whales, one of which was a very large one and spouted up water to a great height.

4^{H}.0^{M}. Dinner. They did not provide an abstinence dinner so we had to take what was set before us. Fare: Soup. Pie. Curry. Roast Goose. Boiled Fowl. Bacon. Vegetables, Potatoes. Carrotts. The potatoes we are eating now are very good being exceedingly dry.

---

223. Peto, Brassey and Betts was a civil engineering partnership between Samuel Morton Peto, Thomas Brassey and Edward Betts. They built a supply and casualty transport railway (Grand Crimean Central Railway) from Balaclava port to the siege lines southeast of Sevastopol in 1855 during the Crimean War. The supply line was considered some to be instrumental in the success of the siege. The firm built civil works in Denmark, France as well as in the UK. In the mid to late 1860's it was active in railway construction in Queensland.
See: Brian Cooke, *The Grand Crimean Central Railway: the story of the railway built by the British at Balaklava during the Crimean War 1854-56*. Cheshire, 1997.

Sweets: Rice Pudding. Tarts gooseberry & Plum. Cheese. Port. Sherry. Ale & Porter.

This afternoon there were a great number of Albatrosses flying about Hopkins and another fellow were firing shot after shot at them and after the 16 shot succeeded in wounding one, it fell in the water. I really pitied it looked so miserable. The whales I have already mentioned were seen about $5^{H}.15^{M}$ PM. Nothing else worthy of remark.

Turned in at $11^{H}.45^{M}$.

Thursday 13

Rose $7^{H}.30^{M}$. Pecksniff as usual till $9^{H}.0^{M}$.

$9^{H}.30^{M}$. Breakfast. Fare: Chops. Mutton. Liver & Bacon. Red herrings. Hash.

10^{H}. Saw lots of Albatrosses, some very large ones following the ship. It is a very fine bird. Body perfectly white and wings grey and exceedingly long. We also saw a very large flock, of a very small kind of gull not a bit larger than a Red Shank, they were on the water. As yet no Cape Pigeons have been seen.

Course S.E.

I had my box No 2 brought up on deck to day to examine if there was mildew amongst the things, I am glad to say that all was safe. I brought down to my cabin some of the shirts, Pocket Handkerchiefs, trousers and towels.

I forgot to say that to day is very fine and a nice Breeze.

O May God give me strength and grace to bear this cross! Well I put up the Journal yesterday, I was getting to melancholy to go on with it.

Lat [*blank*] Long [*blank*].

For dinner we had Soup, Boiled leg mutton, Boiled corn beef, rather too salty, Fowl. Boiled. Bacon rather Pork.[224] Irish Stew. Sweets. Plum Pudding. Tarts. Plum. Gooseberry. Wine. Port. Sherry. Champagne. Ale. Porter. Cheese. Dessert, Almonds Nuts, Figs & raisins.

224. It appears this is what is written, thus inferring that he'd written' Bacon', but should have written 'Pork'.

Plenty of Albatross following the ship. I am glad to say that Hopkins and company have been ordered by the Captain not to fire their guns from the quarter deck, so the poor birds will have peace.

7^{H}. Tea. Afterwards smoked Pipe.

Turned in at $11^{H}.0^{M}$.

Friday 14th

6.20. Rose.

Mass $7^{H}.30^{M}$. Fr McGirr. After Mass usual Pecksniff till 9^{H}.

$9^{H}.30$. Breakfast. Fast. Fare: Ling Boiled. Mutton Chops. Cod roe. Irish Stew. Stirabout & c.

Weather very fine. Breeze about 8 knots. Course S.S.E.

Did nothing particular this Forenoon. Had a chat with the Doctor only think of his telling me as a good joke that in giving physic to one of his patients he made a mistake in giving an aperient when he intended to give the contrary! I laughed like I was ready to drop. I thought that it quite put in the shade 'Edmund and the Particulars'.

There are no Albatross about this morning. Only a few Cape Hens, and a green devil of a bird called a Molly Hawk which is another sort of gull. We are about 5 degrees South of the Cape Good Hope to day. The temperature has become rather cool.

12^{H}. Lunch. Writing my exercise latin, which with reading it to His Grace, occupies me till 3^{H} Office.

4^{H}. Getting ready for Dinner.

$4^{H}.30^{M}$. Dinner. Fare: Pea Soup. Roast Mutton. Boiled Fowl. Bacon. Pork. Boiled Ling for the abstainers. Port & Sherry. Ale. Sweets: Rice Pudding, gooseberry tarts. Cheese.

After dinner on deck.

Saw some sea gulls and a fine Albatross.

Tea at 7^{H} PM. Rosary, Spiritual reading & reading Johnston's *Chemistry of Common Life* at 8.[225]

9^{H}. Night prayers.

$10^{H}.30^{M}$. Rest. Ship's sailing at 10^{H} 10 knots per hour. There will be Mass in the morning.

Saturday 15th

$6^{H}.45^{M}$ - $7^{H}.30^{M}$. Mass. Dr Gregory. Little Hours & reading Scripture with His Grace till $9^{H}0^{M}$.

$9^{H}.30^{M}$. Breakfast. Fare: Mutton chops. Boiled Ham. Hash. Red Herrings. Stirabout.

A very nice breeze this morning. All sails set except the main and fore Royals & Spanker. Ship's sailing Course S.E. Wind N. rate 10 knots per hour.

The only birds about today are a few Cape Hens, Stormy Petrel and some very small gulls the name of which I do not know. The Captain expects a gale of wind as the Barometer has fallen a little. Up to this we have had a splendid passage, the sailors say you might cross

---

225. James Finlay Weir Johnston, Fellow of the Royal Society. (13 September 1796 – 18 September 1855) was a Scottish agricultural chemist.
Born in Paisley, Renfrewshire, Johnston was educated at University of Glasgow, acquired a fortune by his marriage in 1830, and devoted himself to studying chemistry. He visited the chemist J. J. Berzelius in Sweden and was a co-founder of the British Association for the Advancement of Science.
After some years he was chosen as a lecturer in Durham University, but he resided in Edinburgh, and wrote his "Catechism of Agricultural Chemistry" (1844), since translated into most European languages, and his "Chemistry of Common Life" (1853–1855). From 1847, his assistant was Augustus Voelcker who also lectured in agricultural chemistry at Durham University. Johnston died in Durham on 18 September 1855.
Johnston established a grammar school in Durham, which later merged with other local schools to form a single comprehensive school for the area, named Durham Johnston Comprehensive School, thus preserving James Finlay Weir Johnston's name.
Graeme Wynn, "Johnston, James Finlay Weir," in *Dictionary of Canadian Biography*, vol. 8, University of Toronto/Université Laval, 2003–, accessed September 23, 2015, http://www.biographi.ca/en/bio/johnston_james_finlay_weir_8E.html.
http://www.durhamcity.org/bulletin48/johnston.html Accessed 20 September 2015.

the Ocean a dozen times and not get as fine a passage. After having walked a while on deck I came down to my cabin where I read a little of Walter Scott[226] of whose works by the bye I have not as yet read much. But I shall sit at them now.

12. Lunch.

1^{H} till 4 Pecksniff.

It blows pretty fresh this afternoon.

4.30. Dinner. Soup. Mutton roast (all the mutton we have been using is fresh as we have sheep on board which we kill periodically - so is the roast Pork as we have porkers also). Meat Pie, pretty good to day. Boiled Fowl. Pork (Pick'd) in lieu of Bacon. Curry. Sweets: Rice Pudding. Gooseberry & Plum Tarts. Cheese. Ale. Port & Sherry.

After Dinner rollicking on deck for an hour and a half.

Came down to Cuddy to read till 7.10.

Tea. Bread. Salt Butter & Preserves.

8. Rosary and Chemistry, lectures in, with His Grace.

9^{H}. Night prayers.

9.30. On deck smoking till $10^{H}.40^{M}$ when I turn in. The log was heaved at 10^{H}. Rate of sailing about 10½ knots Course S.E. by S. Wind N. by W.

Sunday 16th

$6^{H}.10^{M}$. Rose.

$7^{H}.30^{M}$ Mass. His Grace. Pecksniff till $9^{H}.30^{M}$ when breakfast.

How fortunate that we have Mass so regularly sometimes three times in the week and certainly on every Sunday but two. I assure you that one values more the Most Holy Sacrifice, not that one ought, for difference of circumstances and place ought not to make any difference regarding the estimation in which we hold so solemn a rite, but I may say that when one is bereft of all that is prized on earth, then it appears as if the most Holy Sacrifice comes more as a soothing balm to the true heart than ever one felt it before. And it gives one strength to look on one's lot [?] careless as to what length of time it shall last. For though it is a great happiness to be with His Grace and amongst such holy and good people, yet what on this earth can

226. Sir Walter Scott (1771 – 1832) was a Scottish poet, playwright and novelist.

compensate for the feeling of loneliness experienced by one who is separated from all he loved on this earth.

But may the Holy Will be done.

Well now, to go on with the journal. To commence with breakfast. Fare: Pork. Chops. Broiled ham. Hash. Mince - & c

Morning very fine indeed almost calm scarcely a breath, but there is a long lazy swell which thank God was not sufficient to prevent the celebration of Mass. After breakfast I went on deck for a short time and found that the breeze had got up a little though very little. Fine. Course S.E. by E.

The air is very cold now and the further south we go the colder it will get from the proximity to the Antarctic Circle. Today I think the Lat is 41.45 South.

Many have been the hints thrown out by some to get a sight of this journal but mortal eye, save my own, shall not see it before you my dearest Mother, Brother and Sisters for whom it is written. You will find many faults in it but do not be surprised remember the scatter brain head of him who writes it.

We have great rollicking going on sometimes to beguile the time, picking handkerchiefs out of pockets, and then running after each other to get it again. Some go up the rigging, this however I have not as yet attempted, fearing my head, and I think were I to fall and break my neck, the spree of the thing would scarcely justify me, knowing as I do my weak point.[227] They are now practising one or two pieces in the Cuddy accompaniment on a seraphine, I believe that is the name of it.[228] There are but three of them at it. A Deacon, the performer on the Seraphine and principal singer, a native of Australia and Benedictine, a young ecclesiastical student from Carlow College, and a boy my mate.[229]

Now all chance of meeting a homeward bound ship has vanished. No letter can now be sent till we reach Sydney; I shall get an opportunity of sending this by a gentleman of our party who is bound to Melbourne on business, but who before he returns to England, will call at Sydney and pay a visit to St Marys.

He tells me that he quite envies me, I think I have attended to him before in this journal. His name is Murphy, a paddy of course, but

227. 'spree': excessive indulgence.

228. A 'seraphine' is an obsolete English keyboard reed instrument.

229. Anslem Curtis was the Deacon to whom Athy was referring. The student from Carlow was W Dee.

one who has spent most of his life in England, he has been, I think, but once in Ireland and that many years ago. He has travelled a great deal, having been twice or thrice in Australia. I think he has likewise been in India. He has seen a great deal of the world, I should not be at all surprised to hear of his becoming a monk somewhere or other.

3^{H} -5^{H}. Office (Divine).

$4^{H}.30^{M}$. Dinner. Fare: Soup. Corn beef, boiled. Pork roast. Turkey roast. Mince. Hash. Curry. All the curries are composed of meat and rice mixed up. Bacon, which was not the best, in the portion I got I found something that looked excessively like a maggot: so I put it aside. Vegetables, Carrotts, Potatoes. Sweets. Plum pudding & Sago puddings, Plum & gooseberry Tarts. Cheese. Wines. Port. Sherry. Champagne. Ale. Dessert, Figs, Raisins, Nuts & Almonds.

On dessert days there is a pecksniffian game I suppose is about the right name; viz. if you get an almond with a double kernel you give one to some person, first asking whether he or she as the case may be will take a Philip or Philipun with you. Then the next morning, you must say to the person, if a Lady, good morning Philipun, or Philip if a gent, before the person says it to you. If you succeed in saying it first the person who took the nut must say a Rosary for you or if it is said to you, then you must say the Rosary. I have four in hand.

After dinner exercise till $7^{H}.30^{M}$. Tea.

After tea $8^{H}.0^{M}$ three of us at Rosary with His Grace.

9^{H}. Night prayers and Novena for Xmas. At the end the Litany BVM was sung with accompaniment on Harmonium played by Mother Scholastica, Miss Macarthy. It did very well.

After prayers I went on deck to have my accustomed Pipe.

$11^{H}.30^{M}$. Turned in.

Very little breeze at this hour.

Monday 17

$7^{H}.30^{M}$. Rise.

8^{H}. Pecksniff with His Grace.

$9^{H}.30$. Breakfast. Fare: Curry. Pork Chops. Cold Beef Corn. Dry Hash. Red herrings. Boiled Potatoes.

I won two Philipuns and lost two. So I have two Rosaries to say and I shall have two said for me.

Morning very fine. Capital breeze from N.W. course E.S. E.

A fair wind for Sydney. I forgot to remark that the Southern Cross disappointed me very much. It is a very bad cross turned upside down. I should not have known it had it not been shown to me as it does not much resemble a cross.

Well exercise on deck after breakfast. Came down to Cabin about 12^{H} to take a snooze and at 1^{H} commenced to write the translation of Paradisus, to day's work is easy as it is from Latin to English, but tomorrow's work will be the job, when I shall have to translate again my English to Latin.

From three hours till $4^{H}0^{M}$ time occupied with lessons and Pecksniff.

4^{H} till 4.30 getting ready for dinner.

$4^{H}.30^{M}$. Dinner. Fare: Soup. Roast Pork. Veal Pie. Boiled Fowl. Bacon. Boiled Beef. Curry. Vegetables, Potatoes, Carrotts. Sweets: Rice Pudding. Cherry & Plum Tarts. Cheese. Port. Sherry, Ale.

After dinner exercise. The evening till 7 spent walking about deck, some climbing up the rigging, others playing chess, some reading.

7^{H}. Tea. From 7.30 till 9^{H}, except three of us who at 8^{H} go to the Archbishop to say Rosary read lives of saints and Johnston's *Chemistry of Common Life*, playing chess & draughts and reading.

9^{H}. Night prayers. We have at the conclusion of night prayers, some singing. Sometimes a sung litany B.V.M and some of Faber's hymns.[230] After night prayers I generally take my pipe. Bed at 12^{H}. Mass tomorrow.

---

230. Frederick William Faber, (1814 – 1863)
Faber was born on June 28, 1814, the Son of an Anglican clergyman, at Calverley Vicarage, West Yorkshire, England.
Faber graduated from Balliol College, Oxford and was ordained an Anglican minister, going on to become Rector of Elton in 1843. Three years later, he converted to Roman Catholicism and founded the Brotherhood of St. Philip Neri in King William Street, Strand. He later moved to the Brompton Oratory. Faber published a number of prose works and three volumes of hymns. He died on September 26, 1863 at Brompton, and was buried at Brompton Oratory Church in London. One of his best known hymns is *Faith of Our Fathers*.
http://www.newadvent.org/cathen/05740c.htm
http://www.newliturgicalmovement.org/2013/09/a-tribute-to-fr-frederick-william-faber.html#.VgJah5XouB8
Accessed 20 September 2015.

Tuesday 18

Morn fine very light breeze, course E.S.E.

Rose at 5.30. To day the "Expectatio partus" there was Mass at 7^H.30^M -some of us did our Pecksniff. Pecksniff work continued more or less till 9^H at least with me.[231]

9.30. Breakfast. Fare: Ling boiled. Pork Chops. Hash. Cod roe. Curry, I think. Potatoes. I partook of ling this morning and really found it very good indeed.

10^H. Exercising on deck.

At 11^H I came down to do my things. But I was soon disturbed by news that an Albatross had just been caught by one of the lines. So up I went and there was a large description of gull being hauled in. I do not think it is an Albatross, indeed some say not, it has very long

---

231. Expectatio Partus. In the Marquess of Bute's translation of the Breviary (1879) this Latin is rendered as 'The Blessed Virgin Mary Looking shortly to be Delivered'.
This Feast Day was established in 656 at the Tenth Council of Toledo. There was an ancient law of the Church that prohibited the celebration of feasts during Lent, so the Spanish Church transferred the Feast of the Annunciation from 25 March to the season of Advent. The Toledo council ratified this and fixed the date at 18 December.
When the custom regarding feasts in Lent was no longer observed, the Annunciation came to be celebrated twice in Spain – 25 March and 18 December. The Feast on 18 December was then called 'S. Maria de la O' as after Vespers, the clergy in choir would give voice to a loud and protracted "O" to express the yearning of the universe for the advent of the Redeemer. In Spain, amongst other places, it was called the feast of 'Nuestra Señora de la O'.
It is unknown when the term 'Expectatio Partus' first appeared but the feast was celebrated for over 1000 years. In Spain young baby girls were often given the name 'Maria de la O', indicating how it had become part of the fabric of Catholic life.
By the motu proprio *Ab hinc duos annos* of 23 October 1913, Pope Pius X added reform of the calendar to his breviary reform of 1 November 1911. These changes made it necessary to modify the Roman Missal. They were not implemented until after the First World War and appeared in the 1920 edition of the Missal promulgated by Pius X's successor, Pope Benedict XV. The feast of the Exspectatio partum BVM was removed from December 18 in the calendar for the universal Church and relegated to a supplement for particular dioceses.
Father Rafael Cabezon OP supplied some of this information. See also http://vultus.stblogs.org/?s=feast+of+the+expectation+of, http://www.newadvent.org/cathen/05712a.htm, http://www.newliturgicalmovement.org/2009/11/compendium-of-reforms-of-roman breviary.html#.UjGdWj_4Xms Accessed 20 September 2015.

narrow wings, and the body is not much if anything larger than a large sized Black Backed Gull.

There are some Albatrosses about, but you can easily distinguish them as their whole of the body is quite white, the wings black besides they are much larger than the thing they caught. There are also some Cape Hens. A green devil the name of which I do not know in colour a very light slate. Some. Mother [?]. And little Whale Birds. These last are a small species of Gull, described them some days ago; about the size of a red shank.

I must now set to and translate as it is past one, and I have not written of my translation, English to Latin, a single blessed line as yet and I must present it about $2^{H}.0^{M}$.

Well at $4^{H}.30^{M}$ as usual went to dinner.

Fare: Soup. Roast Pork. Mutton Pie, very bad, woolly. Boiled Fowl, Salt Pork in lieu of bacon. Hash. Boiled Corn beef. Sweets: Sago Pudding. Tarts, green gage & Plum. Cheese. Port & Sherry. Ale.

They administered arsenic to the Albatross or, as it is called now by some a Tommy Hawk or some such name. Others say it is a young albatross. It was a pity to kill as it was not wanted, no one being able to stuff it. There are some very fine ones following us this evening likewise some other birds, curious looking things.

Wednesday 19

$6^{H}.25^{M}$ -$7^{H}.30^{M}$ Mass. Father Cornish OSB in Religion, Mellitus.

Wind N by E. Course S.E. Weather rather wet, rather a heavy swell on. All sails set. Rate at 8^{H} - 10½ knots.

Pecksniff till $9^{H}.30^{M}$. Breakfast (Fast) Fare: Meat & Potatoes. Hash. Cold Corned beef. Meat. Red Herrings.

A few birds following us.

12^{H}. The sea has increased and the vessel rolls a good deal, I have just come off deck, having had a good toss. I came down on my back to the infinite amusement of the bystanders. I really believe that I shall never get sea legs.

Course still S.E. the Barometer has fallen a little, I fear that we shall not witness a real gale now. I suppose that we shall reach Melbourne in about four weeks from this time.

4^{H}.30^{M}. Dinner. Soup. Roast Pork. Pie. Corn Beef. Boiled Fowl. Curry & Rice. Hash. Pork Pickled lieu of bacon. Sweets: Rice Pudding. green gage Tarts. Port, Sherry. Ale, Cheese.

Wind and Rain.

Blowing stiff from S.W.

I forgot to remark that the tea this evening had a very queer flavour I thought it was what we used to call an herb, another thought it partook of the flavour of ants. We afterwards heard that some Rats had been drowned in one of the water barrels, so we have been drinking decoction of Rats.[232] A pleasant idea this.

Thursday 20th

7^{H}.20^{M}. Morning employed as usual.

9^{H}.30. Breakfast. Fare: Pork Chops. Broiled Ham. Cold Corn beef, Dry Hash, Wet ditto. Curry.

A heavy swell on; ship rolling a great deal. A few wild birds such as Albatross and a few small birds the name of which I don't know. They must be some sort of gull as they are so far from land. They are the same birds of which I remarked the other day that they were about the size of a Redshank. Course [*blank*] Wind [*blank*].

The vessel gave such a roll just now as upset the ink bottle. This is the sixth or seventh time that I have spilt my ink.

From 12^{H} to 4^{H} work & Pecksniff as usual.

4.30. Dinner. Fare: Soup. Roast Pork with Cranberries garnishing the dish. Beggars Dish. Roast Goose. Pork, salt, for Bacon. Corn Beef, this dish was so far gone that I could not well make it out so I have taken it for granted. Sweets: Tapiocca Puddings. Cheese. Ale. Wines. Port. Sherry. Champagne. Dessert, Nuts, Almonds, Figs, Raisins.

After dinner swell continued. During dinner every one had now and again to take hold of some dish or bottle to obviate a smash.

These swells are not very pleasant things they come without much wind, though I suppose that they are the consequence of wind in some place or other and after the wind has subsided they roll on till they wear themselves out.

It is well to have seen them as they look rather majestic. But I have now seen so much of them as to have lost at least nearly so the pleasure I took in watching them, so I only feel the inconvenient part of them.

232. 'Decoction' means the extract or essence procured by boiling.

I now wish to see a proper gale or cyclone or something of the sort, for I know that must be a magnificent sight. I should like to see it by day, as by night one would have to stay below.

5^{H}. On deck looking some of them up the rigging, they tried hard to inveigle me up by humbugging me and laughing and all manner of ways but I did not go up. Some day or other for peace sake I suppose I shall have to [?] up.

At 5.30 I came down to write this. They are now practising the Litany BVM in the Cuddy accompaniment, the harmonium, played by Mother Scholastica. The weather is rather cold here now; I find my pilot trousers very comfortable.

Well I shall not be sorry when we land. I have had enough of this sea, confined in this ship is very tiresome. Were it not for the pleasant companions we have I for one should die of dismals.

Log at $6^{H.}$ 10 knots per hour.

There is all the appearance of an approaching gale tonight. The sea rolling on in large dark masses of waves topped with foam. All those learned in the weather prognosticate a gale of wind. The Barometer has fallen a great deal and is still falling.

Came up again at 10^{H} to smoke. This was after prayers & c, at night prayers we sometimes sing the "Litany" BVM and one hymn of Faber's such as "Daily", "Mother of Mercy", "Faith of our Fathers".

Well it is a bright moonlight night with a cloud now and again scudding across the moon, the breeze still rising, and the Capt providing against a gale of wind by shortening sail.

$11^{H}.30^{M}$ turned in.

Wind still rising and Barometer falling. I could not sleep much this night, whatever could be the cause. I lay awake till towards 3^{H}AM. Well of now this cause I can speak about the weather. There was a sort of a gale blowing all night but not a furious one. Not anything like those I have felt at dear Renville, but still a gale that made the ship roll about a great deal; however we were as snug as possible for the Capt had taken in all sails save three.

Friday 21

Rose at $6^{H}.0^{M}$. The swell very heavy, much heavier than last night's gale warranted, I think there must have been a very heavy gale somewhere and that we were only just within its influence. It blows very fresh still. We had hoped to have heard Mass this morning but the ship is rolling too heavily.

Pecksniff till 9^{H}AM.

$9^{H}.30^{M}$. Breakfast. Fare: Boiled ling. Potatoes mashed. Meat. Stirabout. Red Herrings. After breakfast I did not go up as there was nothing to see the wind having very much abated. So I remained in the Cuddy reading.

As usual from 11^{H}.30 till 1 Study & Office.

There are some birds Albatross, Terns, Petrels and some brown queer devils hovering about us.

4.30. Dinner. Fare: Soup. Preserved Salmon. Boiled Ling. Pork. Fowl, boiled. Boiled beef. Sweets, Plum & Rice Puddings. Wine. Port. Sherry. Ale. Cheese.

After Dinner we did nothing particular, as usual draughts & chess playing going on.

From 8^{H} till 9^{H} Rosary & reading with His Grace, (three of us).

9^{H}. Night Prayers. Singing, Litany BVM, Daily, O'Sanctissima.

After Prayers I went up to smoke till $11^{H}.20^{M}$.when I turned in, by this time the weather had moderated a great deal.

$11^{H}.30^{M}$ Bed.

Only fancy what a misfortune happened to my watch. The glass having been broken in some of the falls I got at the commencement of the voyage and having no box wherein to put it, I found in taking it out of my portmanteau this night to wind it the minute hands were broken. Some of the effects of the rolling and pitching.

Saturday 22

$7^{H}.10^{M}$. Rose. Pecksniff as usual.

9^{H}.30. Breakfast. Fare: Pork Chops. Boiled Ham, cold. Corn Beef. Potatoes mashed. Stirabout.

10^{H} to $10^{H}.45^{M}$ on deck nearly all sails set. A ship in the offing which we suppose is likewise bound for Australia. Indeed she must be otherwise she would not be down here. On Course E.S.E. Weather very fine, rather light wind.

Our friends the Albatross, [?] Molly Hawks and other wild devils as usual following.

12 to 4.30. Reading & Pecksniff. At 12.30 there is lunch, 4.30 Dinner. Fare: Roast Pork. Pie. Corn Beef. Bacon. Fowl. I cannot tell the composition of the Pie as I did not partake of it. It is with us more.

6.30 PM and I am writing in my Cabin by the light of day. Well to return to our little dinner there was Curry & Rice. I forgot to begin with Soup. Sweets. Rice Puddings. Plum & gooseberry Tarts. Cheese. Wine. Port. Sherry. Ale.

At $6^{H}.10^{M}$ PM we overhauled the sail we sighted this morning in the offing. She proved to be the Barque *Templeman* from London bound to Hobart Town. She has been out 83 days. [233]

Lat 43.53.

We got close enough to speak her with the Trumpet. She had all sails set and did not appear to have very many on board. The whole strength of our company turned up to see her. Two of our party had a bet as to whether or not her name was on her stern. On closer inspection we read it there: *Templeman – Liverpool.*

She signalised us to request that we would report her at Melbourne to which place we told her we were bound. As also our Lat and number of days out – 52. This not counting the day in which we actually started. It appears that ships never do count the first day in compiling their number of days out.

I forgot to mention that we saw a shoal of porpoises about the vessel to day. They came right under the bows and though we were sailing very fast at least pretty good perhaps between 6 & 7 knots they kept right under ones bow and shot ahead of us every now and then. The second mate succeeded in harpooning one of them but we in the bow were not quick enough in trawling the line, so before we could get him out water the hold was broken.

They say now that we shall be in Melbourne in three weeks from today. Our course is now S.E. at least it was so when I left the deck. Our sails all set. I must go up again now and see what is going on.

---

233. The barque *Templeman* arrived in Hobart town on 23 January 1856, according to a report on page 2 of *Colonial Times* (Hobart, Tasmania), 24 January 1856: "after a protracted passage of 116 days, and bringing a general cargo of *merchandize. Capt. Hewison reports speaking, on the 27th Nov., the barque Sarah Ann, from London to Launceston, out 69 days, also, on Dec 23rd, the ship Phoenix, from Liverpool, to Melbourne, out 45 days.*" *Phoenix* in fact out 52 days at this point.

I assure you that I have seen higher waves off Aran than I have seen all across these oceans.[234] Randal will remember our seeing huge masses of water rising like mountains on the very verge of the horizon there. And again the enormous waves that used to break against the cliffs and send up showers of spray to the very top. Now even in windy weather when the sea is rough you cannot distinguish a wave at all on the horizon.

I believe that our part of the North Atlantic is unequalled by any of the oceans in the majestic grandeur of its storms, indeed all the seamen to whom I have spoken on the subject say as much. The Capt said to me "Why it's always blowing a gale there, winter and summer is all the same".

It was a very pretty sight to see the porpoises playing before the bows of the ship today; they tumbled over again and again and sometimes four or five would leap clean out of the water at a time and give us a full view of them. They were the prettiest marked ones I ever laid eyes on, the back of a greenish hue, underneath white and about five inches of the snout white. I never saw any so marked in the European seas.

At night prayers we sang one of the Oratory hymns 'The Immaculate Conception' to the air of 'What fairy like music'. It sounded extremely well.

At 10^{H} the rate of sailing was 9½ knots per hour. Course S.E.

The people on board the *Templeman* must have envied us seeing how we passed her by and soon got out of sight of her. She must be a terrible tub. She rolled a great deal worse than we did.

I have just come off deck, having had my smoke, it is now $11^{H}.20^{M}$ PM blowing fresh.

Sunday 23

$6^{H}.20^{M}$. Rise. Pecksniff going on till $9^{H}.30^{M}$.

Mass 7.30. Dr Gregory.

Breakfast 9.30. Fare: Mutton chops. Liver & Bacon. Dry Hash – this is a capital dish. Hot Hash of Potatoes & Meat. Mashed Potatoes, baked.

---

234. The Aran Islands are a group of three islands that sit approx 15 kilometres off the Galway coast at the mouth of Galway Bay on the west coast of Ireland. They constitute the barony of Aran in County Galway, Ireland.

10^{H} to 11^{H}. Each one amused himself as he pleased. There were some porpoises about the ship today but the harpoon was rather rickety so it did not act and by the time it was fixed they were gone.

11^{H}. Prayers & Lessons for the Millions.

12^{H}. Lunch. Latitude 43. I really am heartily sick of writing this old journal, it must be so stupid but really I cannot make it better there not being matter and I have not got any inventive faculty.

I have commenced to read W. Scott. I am Paddy-like beginning at the end of the series, Woodstock.[235] I shall spend a great deal of my time henceforth reading.

We are all in high spirits at the approach of the Glorious feast of Christmas. I know that I shall be thinking of you all and how dearly, I should prize, were it permitted, the pleasure of spending that holy time with you all. Randal I know will for he told me so at Liverpool. I wonder what you think of the presents I sent to you and Bessy by him.

4.20. Having had some instructions and finished Office, I have just sat down to day and at this moment it is blowing very fresh there are no clouds the weather looks heavy and has the appearance of an approaching gale. I should very much like to see a gale were it not for the poor fellows who would have to go aloft at the risk of their lives during it.

I have just heard that weather permitting we shall have Midnight Mass.

We have had to shorten sail very much and I still hear the hoarse voice of the Captain giving orders.

It being now just dinner I must shut up.

4.30. Dinner. Fare: Soup. Leg Mutton, boiled. Roast Pork. Roast Turkey. Pork, salt. Potatoes roast & boiled. Sweets: Tapiocca Pudding. Plum & Gooseberry Tarts. Wine. Port. Sherry. Champagne. Ale. Cheese.

After dinner each one employed himself as he pleased.

There is a heavy breeze springing up which carried us, as there is a fog as well to shorten sail still more. Wind N.E., Course E.S.E.

7. Tea. I did not take any today.

Three of us with His Grace saying Rosary, Spiritual reading & reading Johnston's *Chemistry of Common Life*.

9^{H}. Night Pecksniff; after which I had my quiet pipe.

---

235. An historical novel by Sir Walter Scott published in 1826.

10^H. Heaved the log, ship sailing at 8 ½ knots per hour. Turned in at about $11^H.0^M$.

Christmas Eve!

Rose at 7.20. Pecksniff as usual till 9^H.

9.30. Breakfast. Fare: Mutton Chops. Boiled Ham. Curry. Dry Hash. Wet Hash. Mashed Potatoes, baked. Red Herrings. Stirabout.

This morning there is almost a calm like motion being caused by the heaving of a slow swell.

Came down at $11^H.30^M$ to read and translate. Some of the people were fishing for Albatross of which a great many were following us, likewise the Stormy Petrel, some small grey gulls, Molly Hawks, which by the bye the Captain has dubbed Magpie Gulls, by which he means the black gull if there is such a bird.

Randal can look in Buffon or some ornithological work.[236]

These Molly Hawks are brown all over, a lightish brown over the back. Eyes of a bluish slate colour somewhat larger than a black backed gull. The bill similar to that of a large gull, very much turned down at the point. A new bird appeared to day almost as large as an Albatross of a very dark brown; his head white, he did not come very close, so I cannot describe him more exactly.

4.30. Dinner. Fare: Soup. Stirabout. Mutton roast. Boiled Fowl. Bacon. Pork, Salt. Roast Pork. I think, Salmon. Potatoes, Roast & boiled. Sweets: Sago Puddings, Plum & gooseberry Tarts. Cheese. Wines. Port. Sherry. Ale.

5.10. Walking about. Some playing draughts. The weather is very cold now we are so far south; I assure you that great coats are in request. Well the temperature is quite that of Christmas and I am glad of it. I think that a hot Christmas would be very unpleasant.

What an odd thing it appears to be spending the Christmas out here in mid ocean. Away from ones friends and all with which one used to be so familiar. I envy you your happiness. Tomorrow you will be able to have such grand Pecksniff and you will be all together, Randal and all. O! How I wish I could get leave and the means of

---

236. Georges-Louis Leclerc, count de Buffon (1707-1788) was a French naturalist. See http://www.britannica.com/biography/Georges-Louis-Leclerc-comte-de-Buffon Accessed 28 April 2016.

transport, so that by some miracle I could be dropped down among you for that one happy day. But it is better that God's will should be done. He has willed it otherwise, so we should bend our perverse wills to His own noble Will.

I hear that we are to have midnight Mass tonight, so I shall give you a full account of it in a letter, and also in the article for tomorrow.

Our course is S.E. by the compass sometimes S.E. by E., then S.E. by S. Mind in all the entries I have made of our course I have made no allowance for the variation of the compass. Wind is about N.E.

Christmas Day.

12^{H}. Midnight Mass. His Grace. Music. "Venite exultemus Domino", Adeste Fideles, Laudate Dominum.[237, 238, 239] It was a glorious thing to hear Mass and go to Communion at Midnight, on the solitary ocean. Besides they say that we are in the same meridian as the part of the Holy Land in which Our Lord was born.

There was a very good congregation for although it was kept as secret as possible yet somehow or other the steerage and second cabin folks got wind of it and "Paddy" came crushing in.

All of our party except the priests, each of whom are to celebrate, went to Communion and likewise a large number of the Irish. It is really a spiritual feast, and if it is possible to commit, or if there is such a sin, as spiritual gluttony I shall commit it. Father Mellitus Corish will celebrate at $5^{H}.30^{M}$, Father Keatinge at 6^{H}, Father McGee at $6^{H}.30^{M}$, Father Newman $7^{H}\ 0^{M}$, Dr Gregory 7.30, which will be the last.

After Communion at Midnight, thanksgiving finished we ate a few cakes and then laid down, I only threw myself on my bed as I wished to be up in time for the Masses.

The Mass at $6^{H}.30^{M}$ was given out on the eve as the Mass at which any that wished could go to Communion and a great number went, a few likewise went to Communion at $7^{H}.30^{M}$. It is the first time that I have been to Communion at Midnight since I left Hedon.[240]

237. 'Venite Exultemus Domino' are the opening words of Psalm 95.
238. In English 'O Come All Ye Faithful'.
239. Psalm 117.
240. See p 11 Athy Biography for more information.

I suppose that you have had all kinds of Pecksniff and of the richest description in London, and Midnight Mass too. It is so delightful to go to Communion about the very time that our Divine Redeemer came into the world. I do not suppose that any voyages ever had half the opportunity that we have had for "making our souls".

The sea rolled a little yet fortunately not sufficiently to prevent the celebration of the sacred mysteries.

Well I rose at $4^{H}.0^{M}$. At $7^{H}.30^{M}$ there was also some singing. I may say that from 4 till nearly 10^{H} Pecksniff was going on without intermission.

10^{H}. Breakfast. Fare: Mutton Chops. Sort of attempted Irish stew made of some very wooly mutton. Broiled Ham and cold sliced Pork. Baked Potatoes mashed.

$11^{H}.0^{M}$. Prayers in English; one or two of the Victorian Hymns sung. I must say that I do not fancy those hymns at all, at least many of them, there is something Methodistical about them. There are of course some exceptions such for instance as the Hymn to the Sacred Heart which I think beautiful; indeed it would be a great pity to set it to music of the description in which the rest are set.

1^{H}. Lunch. Fare: Sardines. Cheese. Bread & biscuits. I partook of lunch today, and I shall take care not to do so again as I did not feel at all the same; though I did not gormandise to excess. From Lunch till $3^{H}.0^{M}$ doing what each one chose.

3^{H}. Pecksniff, office.

$5^{H}.0^{M}$. Dinner. Fare: Roast leg Pork. Boiled leg mutton. Roast goose. Boiled fowl. Corn Beef. Potatoes boiled & Roast. Sweets: Plum pudding & Tarts. Cheese. Wines. Port. Sherry. Champagne.

The plum pudding was first rate. Dessert, Figs, Raisins, Nuts, Almonds, Plum and other cake.

Just at the conclusion of dinner a message was sent to the Capt that there was a mutiny on board. So he forthwith orders Cutlass, pistols & ball cartridges with which he sallies forth, you never beheld such a laughable scene, the Captain is rather tall but immensely stout, with a corporation like the skipper in Punch [?] at California, his sailors taking to their heels for the Diggins and he vainly shouting after them.

Well up he comes, white with rage with two old rusty horse pistols in one hand and two old and very blunt swords in the other, I am sure that had there been mutiny in reality and had the mutineers seen the weapons, they would rather have been emboldened for I think had the old barkers been fired, from the state in which they were, the possibility is they would have burst and blown the man who fired to where?[241] Blazes.

The mate was also going about with a tremendous black eye and drawing along with him the remains of his coat which in the fray had been torn to smithereens.

But the long and short of it was this: It being Christmas Day, the Captain sold some spirits to the sailors and passengers with which they got glorious and the row took place between decks, the parties being some of the sailors and of the passengers, the ringleader being a passenger an Irishman from Tipperary.

The mate was struck by a sailor, whom he afterwards knocked down with a life preserver. It was after this that he had his eye blackened and his coat torn, by another sailor who thought that his comrade was getting a little too much. And mind religion was at the bottom of it, unmentionable epithets being applied to the priests of our party, not in their presence but amongst the belligerents some of whom were Catholics.

Dr Gregory went down to try and pacify the ship's carpenter who was exceedingly outrageous, and he made a dash at Dr Gregory to try and seize him having at the time an open knife in his hand. I assisted in stopping this fellow when he was breaking away from those who held him, and afterwards was threatened by him, that what would he not do if I did not shove off and not meddle in what did not concern me. As I did not have to exasperate a man who appeared to be almost insane I quietly walked away.

This carpenter when put in his cabin and locked in, took some of his hammers and proceeded to smash his door, but they got him quiet after a while and now again all is peace.

Indeed some of the sailors even who had some little to do with it regret it themselves.

7ᴴ.30ᴹ. Tea and cakes.

9ᴴ. Night prayers sang Dixit Dominus, Laudate Pueri & Magnificat.[242]

9ᴴ.30ᴹ. Grog. We had Snap-Dragons. After all I smoked a pipe on the forecastle and retired at 11ᴴ.40ᴹ.

241. Athy wrote 'the would have burst' but I think he simply missed writing the 'y'.

242. 'Dixit Dominus and Laudate Pueri' are the opening words of Psalms 109 and 112.

Wednesday 26th

Rise at 6^{H}.45^{M}.

7^{H}.30^{M}. Mass. Dr Gregory.

Pecksniff till 9.30. Breakfast. Fare: Pork cutlets. Broiled Ham. Dry Hash. Red Herrings. Corned Beef, cold. Cakes & c.

Course S.E. by S. All sails set W.

At about 11^{H} the day became very wet so we had to stay below. This being Xmas time no lessons going on, only spiritual reading.

12. Lunch. I did not take any to day neither shall I take it again; I had enough last time. I do not think it wholesome to take more meals than one is accustomed to.

The return of sobriety to the belligerents of yesterday evening has restored peace; but some of the sailors say that it is not all over yet that it will rankle for a good time yet.

From 3^{H} till 4^{H} Pecksniff.

4.30. Dinner. Fare: Roast Pork. Pie. Boiled Fowl. Pickled Pork. Corn beef, cold. Hash & c. Sweets: Plum Pudding. Rice. Tarts – Black currants & gooseberry. Wines. Port & Sherry. Cheese. Ale.

After dinner was rather wet.

7.30. Tea & Cakes. Smoking as usual.

9^{H}.0^{M}. Night prayers. Bed at 11^{H}.30^{M}.

We drew lots this evening for the day of arrival at Melbourne. I drew the number 26 so I had nearly the last choice, so for fun sake I chose the 7th February as all the likely dates had been chosen before it came to my turn. We shall please God arrive there now within a fortnight.

I shall be so glad when this voyage is terminated I am heartily sick of it, principally for this reason, that whenever I sit down to do anything a horrible drowsiness comes over me and I am obliged to give way for a short time else I cannot do anything. I have often been more or less so but never to this extent.

I think that the Mr Murphy will become a Pecksniff man like myself; he told me today that he did not think that he should return to England again and he is much given to piety. He is really an exceedingly good man.

Thursday 27

Rose at 7^{H}.20^{M}.

Mass at $7^{H}.30^{M}$. The Archbishop.

Only fancy what a close run I made of it. I had to dress in ten minutes or less. I awoke at $6^{H}.30^{M}$ and feeling very sleepy I said that I would take another doze for a quarter of an hour and then rise as I should have lots of time in three quarters and I did not awake till just 10 minutes before the time; so up I jumped and dressed as fast as I could; neither shaved nor washed and just got in for the epistle. I shall not run such a risk again.

Pecksniff till 9^{H}.

$9^{H}.30^{M}$. Breakfast. Fare: Mutton chops. Broiled Ham. Cold beef corn. Dry Hash. Wet Hash. Sliced Pork, cold. Mashed Potatoes, baked. Bread, butter. Biscuits. Tea.

10^{H}. Ship sailing 8 knots course S.E. Wind S.W. This is about the first time that our cabin has been on the lee side of the ship since we started.

At $11^{H}.30^{M}$ I came down to read and write this stupid journal. However if it does no other good it will make you laugh at the scatterbrained absurdity of it.

Chess & draughts are all the go here but I have not played much at either.

There is also an amusement going on in which I do not partake. There is a baby on board and some of our party are vying with each other in gaining its affections which when they have succeeded whoever the successful party may be carries it triumphantly about.

Now I like babies at distance, but I do not like to venture carrying them about for fear of accidents. Then perhaps I might not succeed in propitiating it so I think it better to leave it alone.[243]

This morning we saw for the first time a brace of Cape pigeons. I think that they belong to the puffin tribe. I have seen them or birds very like them in Galway bay. On the back they are prettily marked with grey & white, and perfectly white underneath. There are very few Albatross with us to day though there are plenty of Petrels and Molly-Hawks.

We are now somewhere off Prince Edward's Islands South of the Cape of Good Hope.

$12^{H}.0^{M}$. Spiritual reading with His Grace.

1^{H}. Lunch.

---

243. 'Propitiating' means to appease, to gain the favour of someone.

Course about S.E. Wind S.W.

3^{H}. Pecksniff.

$4^{H}.30^{M}$. Dinner. Fare: Roast Pork. Boiled Fowl. Bacon. Beef. Curry. Tongue. Potatoes mashed, baked. Sweets: Tapiocca & Sago Puddings. Tarts, Gooseberry & Plum. Wines. Port. Sherry. Champagne. Cheese. Ale.

Dessert, Figs, Nuts, Almonds.

After dinner did nothing worthy of note so I shall cut this short and merely say that I retired after a smoke at $11^{H}.40$.

A couple of Petrels caught today. I was fishing for one with the line belonging to the Doctor who lent it to me for a while. The line merely a bit of yellow silk with a slight weight just to keep it in the water caught them by their getting their legs tangled in it as they flew across it.

I did not succeed in catching a Petrel. I wish I had! But one of these blundering devils of Molly Hawks got entangled in the line and just as I had a strain on the line it gave way. I wished heartily he had been in [?] or somewhere as my line was entirely to light for him.

The Doctor took the line after me and caught two or three, which were let off again with a piece of red silk twisted around their leg.

Friday 28

$6^{H}.20^{M}$.

$7^{H}.30^{M}$. Mass. Dr Gregory. Pecksniff till $9^{H}.30$.

Breakfast. Fare: Boiled Ling. Steamed Pickled Herrings. Hot meats & cold of different kinds. Stirabout.

10^{H}. A heavy breeze came on from N.E. Course S.E. by E. Sea running very high, sent benches and Fowl Coops on the deck flying, also stools and different things in the cabins.

I was up for some time and enjoyed the grand look of the sea exceedingly. Each mountain of water as it rolled, and made the vessel heave again, tended to elevate one's thoughts, and to adore that being whose uncontrollable power sets them in motion.

There was a great deal of rain, so that I could not stop out very long, as I should never be able to dry my clothes again.

I did nothing particular to day. But I hear that from 12^{H} yesterday till 12^{H} to day we made a run of 220 miles. It appears that the ship people count the day from midday to midday.

I took a few whiffs of the pipe.

Lat 45. Long 58.25 about.

It was rather difficult to manage the Divine Office to day as owing to the high seas the Captain ordered dead lights to the stern windows so we could not all say it with His Grace, who has one of the stern cabins.[244] I do not know where the rest said it, but I said it with His Grace.

At dinner to day there was glorious fun. Dishes, bottles and glasses sliding about the table, though fortunately none were smashed. It was most ludicrous to watch the grimaces the Captain made whenever an extra lurch came. He would lay hands on everything in his immediate neighbourhood, lest anything should smash.

After dinner the sea and wind went down very much so we are likely to have a quiet night.

Albatross, Molly Hawk, Petrel, Whale birds, a very small bird, as also a new devil which I had not seen before followed the vessel. Some say that he is a Cape Hen, but if he be a Cape Hen, then the birds that were pointed out as such a fortnight ago are not.

We have shortened sail as it blows fresh.

Saturday 29th

Rose at $8^{H}.20^{M}$. We had hoped to have had Mass to day, but the vessel rolled too much. My Pecksniff with the Archbishop went on as usual.

$9^{H}.30^{M}$. Breakfast. Fare: Rice & Curry. Broiled Ham. Cold corn Beef, sliced. Dry Hash. Red Herrings. Mashed Potatoes, baked.

We had a good deal of work to keep things on the table ship rolling heavily; the swell very high.

Course E.S.E. Wind about N.W. by N.

Distance in last 24 hours 187 sea miles. Lat [*blank*] Long 62.

Very difficult to walk on deck to day the ship rolls so much. But it is a beautiful sight to see these large swells rolling on, then falling over cresting themselves with an immense roll of the whitest foam. There are a few birds following the ship to day.

---

244. A 'dead light' is a strong shutter or plate, fastened over a ship's porthole or cabin window in stormy weather; a thick window set in a ship's side or deck, a strong shutter to fit ports or cabin windows to keep out water.

Only fancy the sailors think that the Petrels are the disembodied spirits of sailors! I suppose of such as have been drowned.

I spent the most part of today in my cabin, at least a good portion of it I was on deck for some time watching the sea.

At 11^{H} rate of sailing 9 knots, at 2^{H} rate of sailing 6 knots. The breeze having slackened a little. I hope that we shall be able to have Mass tomorrow, unless this swell goes down we shall not. However I have great hopes.

Every night there is great playing of cards going on, playing for love, or for nuts and lozenges. I have not played at all. One evening I went down to play and I found that the party wished another to take the hand I was about taking so I gave it up and retired and did not go down again.

It is a very pleasant to hear the sailors singing as they haul the ropes or pump.

4.30. Dinner. Fare: Soup. Roast Pork. Pie á la mode, this extraordinary name frightened me. I might have partaken of it had the name been somewhat simpler. Boiled Fowl. Hash. Pork salt. Potatoes Roast & boiled. Sweets: Rice puddings. Plums, Damson, and Rhubarb tarts, this last I do not know how it is preserved but it is nearly as good as fresh. Cheese. Wines. Port and Sherry. Ale.

After dinner, some playing chess & others Draughts. I was reading.

I fear there will not be Mass tomorrow as this nasty swell still goes on, and they have shortened sail as the Skipper expects a strong gale however I don't place much faith in his prognostications as already he had threatened us with gales four times, which gales never turned up.

Evening playing cards. I was walking on Deck.

9.20. Night prayers. Sang Hymns "Immaculate Conception" and "O Sanctissima".

Wind from N.E. I went to bed at $11^{H}.45^{M}$.

Sunday 30th

No Mass, the ship rolls too much.

Rose at 8. Pecksniff till $9^{H}.15^{M}$ with His Grace.

A nice fresh breeze blowing rather a high sea. Course E.S.E. all sails set 8^{H} A.M. rate of sailing 8½ knots.

$9^{H}.30^{M}$. Breakfast. Fare: Boiled Ling. Mutton Chops. Broiled Ham. Some sort of Wet Hash. Mashed Potatoes baked. Tea & c.

Afterwards doing anything or sitting till 11^{H}. Prayers read by Father Keatinge.

12^{H} Lunch. Log at 12^{H}, 10^{H} per hour.[245]

Hymns sang at prayers Christmas Hymns. 5 from Catholic Hymns. Faith of our Fathers (for England), Oratory hymns, Adeste Fideles.

I shall now read some of Scott. I came down with that intention, but I remembered this bothering journal so I shut up my book in order to get through it.

$4^{H}.30^{M}$. Dinner. Fare: Soup. Leg mutton (boiled). Curry. Beef. Salt Beef. Roast goose. Bacon & Pork, Salt. Sweets: Plum pudding, Tarts, I think gooseberry & Damson. Wines. Port, Sherry & Champagne. Ale. Cheese. Dessert, Figs, Nuts, Almonds.

This evening blowing very hard. Ship rolling heavily, likewise wet. Turned in at 11.15.

Monday 31

8^{H}. I got up. I did not get to sleep during the early part of the night as the rolling was so great, that now and again I almost slipped out of my berth.

Well my usual Pecksniff with His Grace till 9^{H}.

$9^{H}.30^{M}$. Breakfast. Fare: Mutton Chops. I could not see what was at the top end of the table. Dry Hash. Sliced Cold beef, slices. Baked Potatoes mashed.

It blows very hard all day. Sails set Mizzen, Top Sails, Mainsail, Main topsail, Foresail. Fore topsail, the topsails all reefed.

There were some tremendous waves to day. It really was quite a pleasure to stand on deck to look at them. They were very high, several of them used to break a short way from the ship and it was a splendid sight to see them fall over, the crest changing from a dark threatening mass into the most beautiful white amidst which you could see a transparent blue of the most delicate tint possible.

Randal may recollect our having something like it, when we were in Aran; he may remember, when we were standing on a low flat rock on which waves about the height of 12 feet were breaking, though on second thoughts I think those waves at Aran were considerably

245. '10H' This should probable be a 'k' for 'knots'. Looks very much like an 'H'.

higher than that. They used to fall over shortly before they touched the rock thus it was that we saw the white and blue of which I speak.

Well I spent part of the day reading part sleeping and the usual screed of Pecksniff till 4^{H}, at which hour we discovered in the offing a barque "hove to" supposed to be a Sydney whaler. We did not speak her.

4.30. Dinner. Fare: Soup. Shoulder Mutton. Roast. A Pie of some sort. Corn Beef. Boiled Fowl. Pork salt for Bacon. A hash, not very inviting, judging from appearances. Potatoes, mash & Boiled. Carrots. Sweets: Rice Puddings. Gooseberry & Currant Tarts. Cheese & c. Wine, Port, Sherry, Ale.

After dinner we found that we had passed the ship.

Long of today 72.40 E.

Still it blows very hard. Fortunately the day was very fine, blue sky & sun so we saw the sea to perfection. The sailors said it was only half a gale of wind. Course E.S.E. Wind W.

A lot of us stopped up to see out the Old year & the new one in. The sailors made a tremendous row, singing and beating time with sticks on the metal portions of the pumps.

Retired at 1^{H}. 1856.

Tuesday

January 1st

In consequence of the state of the weather we were unable to have Mass today. Morning Pecksniff as usual.

9.30. Breakfast. Fare: Boiled Cod Roe. Broiled Ham. Dry & Wet Hashes. Red Herrings. Mashed Potatoes Baked.

11^{H}. English prayers read by Dr Gregory. Hymns, Oratorian Sung by Miss Ainsworth, Br Anselm & W. Dee.

Nothing particular going on to day. Spare time till $3^{H}.0^{M}$ when it is office time. I say the Office with His Grace. In consequence of the rough weather the dead lights in the Cabins being closed there is not light enough for all so the Benedictines read their Office as best they can.

4.30. Dinner. Fare: Leg Mutton, boiled. Pie. Boiled Fowl. Bacon. Corn Beef. A sort of Stew. Potatoes boiled & Roast. Sweets: Plum Pudding. Tarts some sort of Jam. Wines. Port. Sherry & Champagne. Ale. Cheese. Dessert, Figs. Nuts and Almonds.

I met with a mishap to day after dinner for in larking with a priest, my coat was torn from bottom to top, my Dresscoat.

We had a better tea than usual there being Cakes.

Long to day 77½.

I turned in at about 11^{H} at which time the ship steering S.E. by E. Wind N.N.W.

Wednesday 2

Pecksniff as usual.

9.30. Breakfast. Fare: Boiled Ling. Boiled Ham. Sliced Pork (cold). Mash Potatoes Baked. Dry & Wet Hash.

We shall soon be out of fresh meat seeing as how we have killed the last sheep. Nothing now remains but Pigs. Pork here is very good however it is managed.

There is to be a baptism to day. A young stranger having made his appearance yesterday, some of them want me to stand God Father but as it is with a view of humbug I have refused. [246]

The Longitude to-day is 83.

$4^{H}.30^{M}$. Dinner. Fare: Soup. Boiled Mutton. Pie. Corn Beef. Boiled Fowl. Pork pickled in lieu of Bacon. Some rubbishy hash which I did not taste. Potatoes, roast & boiled, and not of the best quality.

After dinner I remained in my cabin reading. I turned in at $11^{H}.30^{M}$.

Sweets at dinner: Rice Pudding. Gooseberry & Currant Tarts. Wine. Port & Sherry. Ale.

Thursday 3

Pecksniff as usual till 9^{H}.

$9^{H}.30^{M}$. Breakfast. Fare. I am glad today a Pig has been killed so we have fresh Pork chops today.

Boiled Ham. A rascally stew. Pork, pickled, sliced, cold. Sliced Beef, cold. A horrible looking dish of some preserved meat called Roast Beef!!! Stirabout. Tea & c.

246. 'Humbug'. An imposition under fair pretences; to deceive, impose on, cajole.

After breakfast I took a turn on deck for an hour or so, then came down to my cabin and read a little of "The fair maid of Perth".[247]

Studied some Pecksniff and looked over the Latin grammar. At 2^{H}.30 went to His Grace to translate.

3^{H}. Office.

$4^{H}.30^{M}$ Dinner. Fare: Soup. Roast Pork, fresh. A nasty looking Pie of preserved meat. Salt Beef. Boiled Fowl & Pickled Pork. Roast & boiled potatoes as usual. Carrots. Sweets: Tapiocca Pudding. Currant & Gooseberry Tarts. Cheese. Wines. Port. Sherry. Ale. Dessert, Figs. Almonds & Nuts. Excursion on deck till 7^{H}.30. Tea.

I forgot that at $6^{H}.0^{M}$ the baptism took place which has been so much talked of. Dr Gregory officiated, robed in the Benedictine habit & wearing, as Abbot, the Pectoral cross. He was attended by a Benedictine Deacon likewise in the habit.

The child is a girl christened by the name of Mary Elizabeth, the surname is I believe Ryan. I envied the little one, on departing from the font regenerated, the words of the Psalm "Thou hast made him little less than the Angels", comes forcibly into the mind on such occasions. Original sin being washed away, and no actual sins, who can conceive the beauty of such a soul?

And yet I was once the same.

I forgot to mention an incident that occurred yesterday in the afternoon about $1^{H}.30^{M}$. Whilst reading in my cabin with the port hole open and my face close to it, to avail myself of every puff of air, there came a shock which shook the ship, in came a lot of water through my port hole, wet partially my companions bed, and sprinkled me a little; at the same time I heard a great rushing on deck, and a sound as of one falling on the deck, my first exclamation was, there goes some one overboard, the ship was rolling heavily as there was a heavy sea on at the time; I rushed out and as I was just about going up likewise should I meet coming down drenched to the skin but the dear Archbishop.

It appeared that a large wave had struck the ship and dashed up high in the air fell down in a heavy shower first where His Grace was standing wetting him to the skin. The sound I heard at the time was either of the water falling for it came down from a great height or

247. *The Fair Maid of Perth* is a novel written by Sir Walter Scott published in 1828.

some one slipped and fell. Afterwards two or three other waves came over, but unfortunately I was down below and missed seeing them.

To resume to day's journal – the child having been christened, at 7^{H}.30 Tea & Cakes.

Cakes are given as it is Christmas time.

We have full light now till 8^{H} P.M. and have had it these weeks past.

Friday 4th

7^{H}.50^{M}. Pecksniff as usual.

9^{H}.30. Breakfast. Fare: Boiled Ling. Pickled Herrings. Pork Chops. Hash, Dry & Wet. Cold Meats.

Cool now. Very light breeze to day. Course by compass E.S.E. allowing for the variation due E.

Several Albatrosses, Cape Hens & nondescript birds about the ship. Some fellows have lines out hoping to catch some, but they find that "old birds are not caught by chaff".[248]

Through some mistake I did not attend school today.

3^{H}. Office with His Grace, the choir did not come.

Dinner at 4.30. Fare: Soup. Roast Pork. Ling. Boiled Fowl. Salt Pork. Cod Roe. Port. Sherry. Ale. Cheese. Rice Pudding. Rhubarb & Gooseberry Tarts.

This evening there were several porpoises about the ship, one of which they succeeded in harpooning, and getting on board. A curious looking fish he is, a greenish hue on the back sides and snout white. About five feet long. I got a good view of him as I went down on the lower deck or rather, the deck, and elbowed my way through the crowd till I got close up to him.

They are going to give us some to eat on Monday, they say that it is very good eating, I am very curious to taste it.

I suppose that within 25 days from this time we shall arrive at Melbourne. I shall be very glad when I set foot on Terra firma again. It is not easy to do anything on board ship; one gets [?] and then so very sleepy, that one is fit for nothing.

---

248. "old Birds are not caught by chaff": is an old proverb. Old, experienced and wary people are not imposed on easily, or will not bite at every bait.

It is really very cold here now as we get within the influence of the Antarctic regions.

Tea & Cake at $7^{H}.30^{M}$ after which we played whist and other games at cards till $9^{H}.10^{M}$.

Prayers. Sang Litany BVM. A Xmas Hymn "See amongst the winter snows", "O Sanctissima".

$11^{H}.30$ Rest.

Saturday 5th

7.45. Pecksniff.

$9^{H}.30^{M}$. Breakfast. Fare: Pork Chops. Broiled Ham. Hash, Wet. Red Herrings. Meat Cold. Tongue, Pork, Beef.

There was a calm this morning till about $9^{H}.0$ when a breeze sprung up carrying us at about 9 knots which goes on to this moment.

Course Compass E.S.E. that is true E.

Some Albatross and green Devils following in our wake.

12^{H} 0^{M}. Lunch.

Afternoon Pecksniff till $4^{H}.30^{M}$.

Dinner: Fare: Soup. Roast Pork. Pie. Boiled Fowl. Hashes. Corn Beef. Pickled Pork. Port. Sherry. Ale. Cheese.

After dinner heavy squalls came on which lasted the whole evening and night.

Longitude 93, Lat. about 44½. This horrible wind continues I fear that we shall not have Mass tomorrow.

Sunday 6th

In consequence of this rolling of the ship we had not Mass today.

Rose at $7^{H}.50^{M}$. Pecksniff till 9.30.

Breakfast. Fare: Pork Chops. Broiled Ham. Wet Hash. Dry Hash. Sliced Corn beef & Pork. Cold Stirabout. Mashed Potatoes baked.

After breakfast sauntered about till $11^{H}.0^{M}$ AM when we had Prayers on the Million and a long winded Sermon, I do not know the name of the Author. Sang the Adeste Fideles, Alma Redemptoris.

There is a heavy breeze today causing a great swell at breakfast time every now and again we had to hold hard or some of the dishes would have been swept clear off the table. It makes me laugh tremendously to see the grimaces the Captain makes during these lurches. He appears to be in the most intense agony, and in reality I believe he is so, mentally, for he has some share in the profits and losses of this trip. So it stands him upon to have as few smashes as possible.

From 12^{H} Noon yesterday till the same hour today we have come 232 miles. We are almost in the 99 degree E Longitude and 43 S Latitude.

I partook of lunch to day. A little sardine which by the bye nearly made me sick, some cheese & bread and a stoop of Ale.[249]

I told you before I believe that His Grace gave me a dispensation for Ale.

3^{H} Divine Office. His Grace and I said it together. The others said it as they could. His Grace always makes me say the office with Him to train me before I figure in choir at St Mary's. I shall be delighted when I am put in harness.

$4^{H}.30^{M}$. Dinner. Fare: Soup. Pie preserved meat. Roast Pork. Roast Turkey. Pickled Pork. Corn beef. Rhubarb & Gooseberry Tarts. Plum Pudding. Port. Sherry. Champagne. Ale. Cheese. Dessert, Figs, Almonds, Nuts.

After dinner walking on deck for a while, afterwards reading.

$7^{H}.30^{M}$. Tea & Cakes. I forgot to say that the lurching of the vessel made the dishes rattle about the table which kept the poor Captain in hot water during the whole time.

$9^{H}.0^{M}$. Night prayers, we sang the litany BVM & Hymn for the feast Epiphany, Laudate Pueri & Magnificat. After all was over I took a tumbler of Beer and smoked my pipe and retired at $11^{H}.30^{M}$.

Monday 7th

Rose at 8^{H}. Pecksniff as usual.

9.30. Breakfast. Fare: Curry and Rice. Broiled Ham. Dry Hash and Stew. Cold beef and Pork salt, Sliced. Mashed Potatoes baked. Red Herrings.

A small portion of the Porpoise was sent to table by the first mate to give us a taste of it. It was prepared and cooked by himself and

249. A 'stoop/stoup' is a drinking vessel; a vessel for liquids; a small but indefinite measure of liquid, ranging from half a pint (approx 285 ml) to two quarts (2.26L).

really I do not know when I tasted anything I liked better, it looked like a black pudding and tasted very much the same, minced up seasoned with pepper and salt.

As usual I went on with my latin translation with His Grace.

Longitude to day 103.

There were a set of Goths to day from the second Cabin peppering away at those unfortunate Albatrosses of which they missed a great number and succeeded in wounding a few and there were the poor things in the water in pain for no earthly good. I think it is the most cruel proceeding I ever witnessed. I could excuse it could they get the birds in order to stuff them, or even if they were sure of killing them; but as it is I think it inexcusable.

The breeze was very light to day and the swell subsiding. The greater part of the day we were making but from 5 to 7 knots.

4.30. Dinner before which, as usual, I recited Matins and Lauds with His Grace.

Dinner. Fare: Soup. Roast Pork. Pigs Head. Boiled Fowl. Pickled Pork by way of bacon and precious bad stuff it is. Preserved meat pie. Corn beef. Wines, Port & Sherry. Ale. Cheese.

After dinner I took exercise for a while smoked a pipe in the Galley the name by which the kitchen goes, had a chat with the old cook a regular Sambo from the West Indies.

Others of our party were playing draughts. I came down afterwards to read some of Walter Scott. I have not read a line of [?], or [?]. I shall reserve that for St Mary's if I am allowed to read them there.

Poor Dr Gregory has had severe attacks of rheumatism he has been laid up for the last few days.

$7^{H}.30^{M}$. Tea & Cakes. After which we usually play cards, Whist parties and a round game.

9. Night prayers. Sang Litany. The hymn Daily 3rd part, O Sanctissima.

Smoked my pipe after all and turned in at 11^{H} at which hour I sat down awhile to write up this plaguy journal.[250] It is expected now that we shall arrive in Melbourne on next Thursday or Friday week. But I think it rather doubtful. I say on next Sunday or Monday week.

250. 'plaguy'. harassing, troublesome, tormenting, vexing – often used in annoyance as an intensive.

The journal will not be worth the postage home; I am in doubt whether or not I shall send it. I thought once that I should have had an opportunity of sending it by one of our party a W. Murphy, but he does not as yet know whether he will return or not just yet. He is a very nice person, should he return I shall give him a letter of introduction to you.

Tuesday 8

8^{H}. Rose. Pecksniff as usual till $9^{H}.30^{M}$.

Breakfast Fare: Boiled Ling. Pork Chops. Hash. Mashed Potatoes baked. Tea & c.

Afterwards I went up and exercised on deck till 11^{H} when I came down to prepare my translations for His Grace. But first I made ½ hours [?] then read some of Waverley, "Fair Maid of Perth".[251]

12^{H}. Lunch. I did not take any, but I went to the Galley afterwards to take a pipe; somehow or other I found W. Blake, the old cook, that is his name in rather a bad humour.[252] It's odd to hear that name on board the *Phoenix* applied to a fellow as black as the pots.

Well I went to the Archbishop at 2.15. At 3^{H} we recited Matins and Lauds. The Nuns and Father Mellitus came to day. Dr Gregory was unable on account of his rheumatism. After Office I had to read the Psalms, with notes till $4^{H}.30^{M}$.

Dinner. Fare: Soup. Roast Pork. Preserved Meat Pie. Corn Beef. Boiled Fowl. Pork. Curry. Sweets. Tapiocca Puddings. Rhubarb & Currant tarts. Cheese. Port. Sherry. Ale.

After dinner I did nothing particular till about $6^{H}.30$ when I read some of Walter Scott.

7.15. Tea & Cakes.

8^{H}. Playing cards till 9^{H}.

Night prayers. Sang Litany BVM and Faith of our Fathers. I must say that the more of these English hymns I hear the less I like them. They sound very Methodistical.

---

251. These are two of Sir Walter Scott's novels.

252. Blake, Thos., the ship's Cook, aged 52. in the record of names arriving in Sydney on the *Phoenix* on Jan 28, 1856. See http://mariners.records.nsw.gov.au/1856/01/085pho.htm Accessed 20 September 2015.

At 10^{H} went on deck to smoke, when the greatest incident of to day occurred. Whilst in the wheel house, I heard some one near the gunwale, at a very dangerous part crying out in a frantic manner for Mr Hales, the mate, but just before the voice there was a smash of glass. I ran up and then saw two people struggling in a fearful manner close to the edge of the ship, at a place where it was an easy matter to heave a fellow overboard.

When Hales came up he had some work to separate them, when it turned out to be the Ship's Purser and First Steward who had a row and the Purser being the stronger of the twosome that he intended to throw the Steward overboard and go overboard himself with him.

That he came on board the ship with the character of an honest man, and that the steward had tried to destroy it. That it was the trial between a clear conscience and a guilty one, "let us both go overboard together and answer it in the other world". There must have been something between them that as yet we know nothing of but which will come out later.

The Captain declares that he will give the Purser up to the Authorities at Melbourne.

I thought at first that the Purser was drunk; but on seeing him afterwards come aft and steer the ship I altered my opinion for had he been so, he could not have steered.

The Steward declared he does not to this moment [*know*] what he has against him.[253] That when he sprung out and caught him by the collar, he said him "what are you doing?" Do you know who you have collard!

The Purser said he knew very well, that he was just the fellow wanted. And that he would heave him overboard.

I forgot to say that as soon as W. Hales found out who they were that were struggling, he said to the Purser what do you want cousin? Leave this man alone.

He answered "I want to go overboard with this Fellow". Both the Purser and the Steward are Irish.

You never heard such cursing and such language. Such unseemly sounds do not become this Pecksniffian ship. I hope that I shall not have to be brought forward as evidence at Melbourne if they go to law.

253. The word 'know' was not written in the Journal but seems to be needed for the sentence to make sense.

Wednesday 9th

Pecksniff as usual.

9^{H}.30^{M}. Breakfast. Fare: Broiled Ham. Cold Pork, Sliced. Hash. Mashed Potatoes baked. Tea & c.

11^{H}. Came down to write journal which by the way has taken up an immensity of my time for being a slow scrivener with a very bad memory it occupies twice the time with me that it would with any one else.

12^{H}. From the same hour yesterday up to to day we came 220 miles. Long 112½. Average some what better than 9 knots per hour. Sailing by compas E.S.E.[254] The variation of the compas being two points to the Eastward makes our real course E to 1 point to the S.

The Steward who last night had been mauled by the purser has not appeared to day; not that he is compelled from the injuries to lay up and I hear that he has only a few scratches on his face. But you know that Paddy in such cases makes mountains of molehills.

There is one priest here who is such an Irishman that you cannot say the slightest thing in disparagement of them but he has his horns out at once. I am one I thought that I was Irish enough but because I do not turn every thing they do into virtues we do not agree.

He even defends the fact of no priests having gone from Ireland to the Crimea. And lays claim to the English priests of Irish name who have gone out. I understand him to say that the priests from Ireland did quite right in not going. That the English brought on the war and let them provide for the spiritual as well as temporal. That Almighty God would take care of the Irish who fell there and save them. He is all on the Russian side, hoping that they may win. He picked this Irish up in Rome where he says the feeling is all Russian.

Thursday 10

6^{H}.20^{M}.

7^{H}.30^{M}. Mass. The Archbishop.

Pecksniffian ordinary till 9^{H}.30^{M}.

254. Word is written in Journal with one 's'. The word 'compass' is derived from the Old French 'compas'.

Breakfast. Fare: Pork chops. Broiled Ham. Cold meats sliced. Beef. Pork. Dry hash. Stew, Mutton & Rubbish. Potatoes mashed baked. Tea & c.

After breakfast as usual till 10.30 when I came down to read & study. I find my head very dull, the fact is my brains have got very, very rusty and whether or not I shall ever be able to clear them again remains to be seen. All my prayers are now directed to this end. I am so very forgetful.

12^{H}. Lunch.

Distance since 12^{H} yesternoon [*blank*].

2^{H}. Reading to His Grace.

3^{H}. Office as usual.

4.30. Dinner. Fare: Pigs head boiled. Preserved meat pie. Corn Beef. Tongue. Pork Pickled. Boiled Fowl. Potatoes mash & Boiled. Only fancy they garnish the pickled pork with Carrots.

There were some nice pickles on the table. By the way I made an awful mistake some time ago, there was a bottle of very tempting pickles on the table, out of which I helped myself; I afterwards discovered that it was private property. I thought that it belonged to the Mess.

After dinner on deck as usual till about 6^{H}. Came down to read.

6.45. Went with Br Curtis and W. Dee to spiritual reading with His Grace.

$7^{H}.30^{M}$. Tea & Cakes. After which I took my pipe, to which I shall soon have to bid a long farewell so I must make the best of my time. I smoked in the Steward's berth which is in one of the houses on deck.

$9^{H}.0^{M}$. Night prayers. Sang the Litany BVM Hymn Oratorian, "Immaculate Conception", O Sanctissima.

10^{H}. On deck, smoking till 11^{H}. Ship sailing then 10 knots per hour. We shall at this rate probably reach Melbourne on Wednesday or Thursday next.

There are some wild birds following us to day. But I suppose that in two or three days more we shall lose them.

We are now under the lee of Australia but it is five or six hundred miles to the N. Ship's course to day was nearly true E a point to the S.

I hear that the Purser has settled the row he had the other day with the Steward. It is well for him he did so for there was the clearest evidence of an attempt to murder against him; his dragging the poor fellow from the entrance of the Cuddy to the gunwale, and then saying that he intended to heave him overboard and suicide, by his saying that he would go overboard himself with him.

I shall see Father Parsons in all probability at Melbourne where I suppose we shall stop a couple of days. I may also see "plain Mary" who I suppose is located somewhere there.

Friday 11

5^{H}.15M. Rose as it was settled last night we were to have Mass at 7^{H}.0^{M} and I wanted to do Pecksniff. But unfortunately the breeze was too high there was too much motion so we were disappointed. I discovered this at about 6^{H}.20^{M} or 30^{M} so I laid down again as I was till 8^{H}.10^{M} when I went through the usual pecksniff.

Ship sailing well this morning 10 knots per hour.

9.30. Breakfast. Fare: Cod roe. Ling. Sliced meats. Tongue. Beef & Pork, pickled. Potatoes mashed. Tea & c.

Ships course due E 1 point N.

10^{H}. as usual on deck.

11^{H}. to cabin to write this journal and read.

12^{H}. Long [*blank*]. 11 knots per hour.

12^{H} Noon to 12^{H} Noon to day distance 232. The distances are always recorded in knots one of which as I before said is equal to an Irish mile.

Afternoon till 2^{H}.15^{M} remained in my cabin; at this hour went to His Grace as usual. I did not remain long as Dr Gregory came to him on business, so I had to "hook it" as they say. Poor Dr Gregory is severely attacked with Rheumatism which he bears admirably you can read pain in his countenance but that is all, he neither complains nor murmurs.

4^{H}.30^{M}. Dinner. Fare: Soup. Preserved Salmon. Ling. Roast Pork. Boiled Fowl. Pickled Pork. Tongue. Potatoes roast & boiled. Sweets: Rice Pudding. Tarts, Gooseberry & Damson. Wine. Port. Sherry. Ale. Cheese.

After Dinner exercise & Pipe till 6^{H}.30^{M} when three of us went to His Grace to say Rosary. Spiritual Reading. Chemistry.

7^{H}.30^{M}. Tea & Cakes. Whist till 9.15 Prayers after which smoked till 10^{H} then I turned in.

Saturday 12

8^{H}. Pecksniff as usual.

Today I am overpowered with sleep, whatever is the reason. Whilst I am writing this I can scarcely keep my eyes open though it is $12^{H}.0^{M}$ or rather 1^{H}.

Breakfast: Pork Chops. Broiled Ham. Dry Hash. Red herrings. Slices of cold Pork. Mashed Potatoes baked. Tea & c. Afterwards went on deck for a short while then came down to read Scott and write this.

Every one is now speculating on the day of our arrival at Melbourne some say on Tuesday next others Wednesday, Thursday & Friday. I am anxious about it as I have a bet of $^{S}10$ that she will not arrive there within 80 days from the day she left Liverpool, This bet I made nearly two months ago.

We set sail at about 10^{H} 27 October so it is that

Oct	4
Nov	30
D	31
J	12
	77 up to today.

12^{H} – 1^{H}. Lunch. I did not partake. The whole of this evening was spent in doing Pecksniff.

4.30. Dinner. Fare: Roast Pork. Preserved Meat Pie. Salt beef & Pork. Rice Curry with preserved meat, of which the curry is always composed, and detestable stuff it is. Sweets: Rice Puddings, Gooseberry & some other fruit Tart. Port. Sherry. Ale. Cheese & c.

After dinner as usual.

7. Tea & Cakes.

9^{H}. Night prayers. Sung. Litany BVM Adeste Fideles, Bethlehem hymns, the form the "Old Cow died of ".

Smoked on deck this is almost my last Pipe.

Sunday 13

$5^{H}.30^{M}$. Mass at $7^{H}.10^{M}$.

Thank God we were able to have Mass to day. Celebrant F. Keating. A large number of communicants - Deo Gratias. After Thanksgiving went to His Grace to say Little Hours.

$9^{H}.30^{M}$. Breakfast. Fare: Pork Chops. Broiled ham. Dry Hash. Stew. Potatoes, mashed baked. Cold Meats. Tea & c

11^{H}. Prayers and long winded Sermon for the Million!! I don't know whose sermon it was, Father Keatinge officiated. I think the sermon book belongs to the Nuns.

12. Lunch.

I was doing different things till 3 Office.

$4^{H}.30$. Dinner. Fare: Roast Pork. Pigs head boiled. Boiled Fowl. Tongue. Salt Pork. Potatoes Roast & boiled. Sweets. Plum puddings, these are about the best things we get in the sweet line, they are not too rich. Tarts of some sort. Wines. Port & Sherry. No Champagne. Ale. Cheese. Dessert, Nuts and Almonds. Figs.

I believe there is to be Mass again tomorrow; a Feast of the Order S.B. St Bennet Biscob.[255]

There are rumours of the Doctor of the ship being hooked with a law suit.

This is the story – A Scotchman by name Smith has a sore leg, which was caused by a large box falling on it during a lurch the ship got when crossing the bay of Biscay. Well the Doctor, who is a right good fellow, I believe I told you before he is a brother in law of Waterton's, attended this fellow, but before he had him three days under treatment, he pitch forked him away for the sake of a fellow, who told him that he could cure him in a week! So of course the Ship's Dr did not interfere. Here he is now with his sore leg unhealed, for this chap who undertook to cure him put some awful stuff on it which burned right down to the bone. So now it is still bad with him.

I took my last Pipe this evening. I shall not smoke anymore.

I expect that we shall be at Melbourne on Thursday. So I shall win my bet but I shall lose another as a fortnight ago I made a bet that we should not be there on Friday next. I am getting very stupid my head is always doldorized now. Were it not for this I should have made this

255. Benedict Biscop. Born Biscop Baducing (c. 628 – 690).In recent times his Feast Day is celebrated on January 12, He is the Patron of English Benedictines, musicians, painters, and the City of Sunderland, England. See http://www.catholic.org/saints/saint.php?saint_id=929 Accessed 20 September 2015.

Diary much more interesting. I assure you that it is a great source of mortification for me at times.

Monday 14th

$5^{H}.50^{M}$. $7^{H}.15^{M}$ Mass. The Archbishop.

Pecksniff all the morning.

God be praised! If he has not blessed me with a bright head it is so much the better for me. I am already of such a vain disposition, a sure sign of folly, that were my vanity not counteracted by some defect that is brought home to me so continually, there would be no bearing with me not that I mean by that to insinuate that I have no other defects far from it, for alas I have too many. But the defect of an obtuse intellect comes across one so often that at length it must succeed in reducing the vice I have just named. If I am but knowing enough to reach heaven that is all I care about. Though I admire and prize knowledge highly, yet if it is not for me I have no business to repine. An Omniscient Creator made me and though I believe that I am to blame for not having cultivated what He has given me; yet I believe that naturally I am deficient compared to others.

Breakfast $9^{H}.30^{M}$. Cod Roe. Pork Chops. Cold Tongue. Cold Pork Salt. Potatoes Mashed. Dry Hash. Tea & c.

They are washing and cleaning up the ship in great style, as they expect to reach Melbourne on Wednesday next. This is a holyday on account of it's being St Benedict Biscob a Benedictine Abbot.

Tuesday 15th

8 Rose. Pecksniff as usual.

$9^{H}.30^{M}$. Breakfast. Fare: Pork Chops. Broiled Ham. Stew. Cold Meats. Tea & c. Potatoes Mashed baked.

11^{H}. Reading & translation.

12^{H}. Lunch. I did not partake of lunch.

Distance for the last: 218 miles.

3^{H}. Divine Office.

As usual 4.30 Dinner. Fare: Pigs Head. Roast Pork. Tongue. Curry as usual of rice and preserved meat. (I forgot the first course Soup).

A preserved meat pie. Potatoes Roast & boiled. Sweets: Tapiocca puddings. Some kind of Tarts. Cheese. Wine. Port. Sherry. Ale.

After dinner took a turn on deck till 6^{H}.0^{M} when I came down and wrote this.

At 6^{H}.30^{M} I shall have to go to the Archbishop's for an hour or so.

Nothing of any note happened to day. There were a few birds about as usual yesterday. For the first time we were visited by the black Albatross, today also we had him about the ship.

It is now said that we shall reach Melbourne on Thursday. I hope such may be the case. But I really entertain doubts about as it was not said in a positive way.

Sighted Land at 2^{H}.30^{M}[256]

Wednesday 16th

8.15. Pecksniff as usual. They say we shall see land today, but as yet there is no appearance of it. I hope we may. I am tired of looking at this eternal sky & water.

9.30. Breakfast. Fare: Pork Chops. Broiled Ham. Hash. Herrings, red. Cold Meat. Mashed Potatoes baked.

After breakfast exercised on deck a while then came down to do several things in my cabin among which to prepare my translation for His Grace occupied a prominent place.

12^{H}.45^{M}. I took a glass of ale and a mouthful of herring.

Distance since 12 yesterday 170^{m}. Long 42½.

After lunch there was a rumour that land was sighted. But I did not go up. I had to finish my translation.

I lost a little medal some two months ago, which thank God I found to day, when I was moving the boxes so as to permit the Stewardess to clean out the cabin. It is the medal of the "Rosary of the Crown" of the B.V. M. given me at [?]. This is the second time I have lost and found it. I hope I shall not lose it again.

2^{H}. As usual to the Archbishop to read translation.

He let me go at 2^{H}.40^{M} so I went on deck and saw Land distinctly in the offing. What a relief to one's eyes; and also to one's mind to know that this long journey will soon come to an end. The land is becoming more distinct every moment.

256. This was written at the top of the page on the day that Athy spied land.

3^{H}. Office as usual.

$4^{H}.0^{M}$. Can now very distinctly see the land which is very high in one part, it is about N.E from where we now are at a distance of nine or ten miles. The top of the highest part is crowned with a forest apparently.

4^{H}.40. Dinner. Fare: Roast Pork. Preserved Meat Pie. ($1^{\#}$ Soup). Corn Beef. Irish Stew. Tongue. Boiled Fowl. Salt Pork and Bacon. Potatoes roast & boiled. Sweets: Rice Pudding. Rhubarb & Gooseberry Tarts. Wine. Port & Sherry. Ale. Cheese & c.

After dinner went up and saw the land very distinctly. We now can discern with the eye that the summit of the highest land is crowned with foliage. It is about as high as the Black head range.[257]

There is a steamer sailing close under the hills supposed to be bound for Adelaide. I should say that the land is about 6 or 7 miles, perhaps 8 or 9 miles distant from us. I am writing this at $6^{H}.0^{M}$ PM.

We have four or five lines out in hopes of catching a queer fish called Barracouta I wonder what he is like. The Captain tells me that it much resembles a Hake. The hook used is about the size of a Hake hook or Cod Hook. The bait a set of rags of the most gaudy colours around wire. The bait floats on the surface there being no weight attached and as the ship is going at 6 or 7 knots it comes quite over water.

6.30. Rosary & Spiritual reading with His Grace.

At about 7^{H} or between 7 to 8 passed Cape Otway which is 90 miles from Sydney on which is placed a revolving light.[258] We are now sailing within 4 or 5 miles of land.

Cards till 9^{H}. Night prayers. Sang Hymns Oratorian, The Angel Guardian & O Sanctissima. [259]

10^{H}. Went on deck beautiful moonlight night, the reflection of the moon on the water and the light cast on the hills is beautiful.

At 10^{H}.45 a light seen ahead which turned out to be a steamer.

We expect to reach Melbourne before noon tomorrow.

257. Black Head Range is a mountain range at the head of Galway Bay and stands almost 200 metres high.

258. Athy would have meant to write 'Melbourne'.

259. 'Oratoriane' seems to be the word written here.

Thursday 17

$3^{H}.10^{M}$. Rose as I could not sleep in consequence of the noise and turmoil going on over my head on deck. I found that it was caused by a very violent breeze which had sprung up suddenly so much so as to make it necessary to come about and stand out to sea again. The wind from S.W.

After our tack, the first we have made since we left the Smalls, islands or rocks at the mouth of Bristol Channel, we stand S.

It is now certain that we shall not get to Melbourne to day; it appears that there was some mistake in the middle watch as about $4^{H}.0^{M}$ we passed the heads at Port Philip, being the entrance to Melbourne. I do not as yet known why we could not have entered with a S.W. Breeze.

We have caught a good number of Barracouta to-day. It is a most queer looking fish in colour very much like a hake, the head a good deal sharper than that of the hake and the tail like

(*here an illustration*)

the large ones are about the size of a small Hake. There are no less than six lines out astern, which are always getting foul of each other.

The Breeze still continues very heavy.

5^{H}. We have been obliged to take in ever so much sail and likewise to take in reefs. I assure you we were in no very pleasant position this morning being at one time rather too close to an ugly looking reef.

Well we were obliged to stand out to sea again as it blew so very hard, we were afraid to venture on entering the harbour but about 3^{H} the weather moderated somewhat.

Well we have had some sport to day catching these Barracoutas and we had one of them for breakfast and right good they are. Also at dinner we had some.

I really forget now the Fare, as I am writing this on Monday night 21st Jan. I am very forgetful.

Well at about six o'clock we took the Pilot on board and entered Port Philip heads between that and 8.30 at about which time we came to anchor ahead of the light house, not intending to proceed over to Melbourne till morning. From Port Philip light to which town is a distance of 35 or 40 miles.

The Pilot is a scotchman, very much browned, I suppose by the Australian Sun, and is a quite dapper fellow with moustaches, wearing one of those short morning coats black trousers and [?] Japan boots.

As soon as he came on board he was surrounded by a whole host of us putting questions to him, but so plagued was he that he at length said, "Wait gentlemen till I get the sails full and the ship underway and then I'll talk to you". The Pilot boat is a schooner of about 90 Tons, had been a yacht belonging I believe to Lord Byron.

There were a whole lot of fellows on board of her some with straw hats and others with glazed sailor hats, lounging elegantly at the gunwale, and staring at us. I heard afterwards that they were all pilots waiting their turn. They take the ships by turn.

Well inside the heads there is a very nice anchorage, almost completely protected by headlands from the heavy swell of the ocean.

Friday 18

Rose at 8. The Pecksniff as usual.

We have been underway since a very early hour this morning. The shore on each sides appear to be very sandy and of course barren. We came to anchor either at $10^{H}.30^{M}$ or 11^{H}.

Well we are, at least a good number of us determined to go on shore. I shall go as it is proper to see every part of the new country that one can. The harbour is a very fine one. At least it can be made so in the course of time at present there is only two piers or more properly landing places one of which that at Sundreach is of wood, another at Williamstown of [*blank*].[260]

Well all the Ship's company are decked out in their best togging steerage passengers and all, of which lot we shall lose I think over a hundred and fifty. Amongst them Hopkins and a scotchman by name Smith, who has been threatening law proceedings against the Capt for some boxes or things falling over his leg and hurting same.

260. 'Sundreach' is as written, phonetic spelling perhaps for 'Sandridge'.
Sandridge is now known as Port Melbourne, a suburb of Melbourne, 5 km south-west of the city's Central Business District. The suburb is bordered by the shores of Hobsons Bay and the lower reaches of the Yarra River. Assistance with Information thanks to Fr Colin Fowler OP.

Much chance he has of success! I know I would not give him 6^d for his chance.

Well all kinds of geniuses are coming on board in the shape of government officers. One of them was a great swell with jet black hair a cap with a grand gold crown on it. He had a strong look of Jim Ryan. He took from the Capt the number of passengers and other things.

Also the first Lieutenant of H.M. Ship *Electra*, stationed here came to pay a visit to His Grace.

Well at about 11.30 or 12.30 I and a party left the ship for shore. We went in a little sport sail boat belonging to the harbour; from the ship to the landing place is a distance of three or four miles for which we had to pay 3 bob per head for the hire of boat. Well we landed on a fine long wooden, I can scarcely call it a pier, temporary quay I suppose is a more appropriate name and proceeded forthwith to the railway station, which takes us to Melbourne for you remember that we landed at Sundreach.

When we arrived at the station we found a number of priests waiting, hoping that His Grace had come ashore in the boat with us, however he did not. They told us that "the Bishop of this Diocese" had gone to the *Phoenix* to pay his respects. Some of the priests came with us and took us to the Presbytery where we were most hospitably received.

I met poor W. Parsons there what a changed man he is. He has been in a very bad state of health he told me for the last two years. I do not think he will live long. He did not know me at first, but when I told him my name and mentioned circumstances to him which I knew would refresh his memory, he seemed greatly agitated and unable to speak for some time & has since told me that I gave him a great shock in which I can well understand his health being so weak.

When I remember the active man he was in the halcyon days of Hedon and see him now a perfect wreck I think it almost a pity that I went to see him at all. But I could not pass by one to whom under God I owe so much; without taking one look at him. We talked a good deal about Hedon, our old friends there and the retreat I went through there and which W. Parsons said, was the one which brought me out here. His spirits seem completely gone, and no wonder. May those who so foully wronged him repent while there is yet time, or fearful will be their fate.

Well as soon as we had taken a mouthful one of the priests escorted us through Melbourne to show us the lions;[261] I must say that the progress made by this city since first founded greatly astonished me. There are about one hundred and twenty thousand inhabitants. The streets are fine and wide; but there is one drawback the great quantity of dry sand on them and which with the least wind blows about and fairly blinds you.

The exhibition building is also very fine. Built in the style of that class of buildings called crystal palaces. I bought a cigar or two though really very good ones and cheap enough.

Dear Rev. Cicerow took us to see the seminary, which promises to be a very fine building; it is not half finished. In the garden he had a tame kangaroo, a queer looking animal it is. And in his room an Australian bird called a 'Moe Pok' of the owl species.[262] A moping bird.

Well we afterwards walked about the town till $4^{H}.30^{M}$ when we went to the Presbytery to dinner. The church is a pretty one the ceiling being of Cedar and nicely carved.[263] It is got up in the Pugin style; it is Cruciform. They are now building a large chapel to it. The wall behind the Altar is done with blue paper with gold stars. They have a very fine statue of the Blessed Virgin, and sculptured by, I believe, a Melbourne man, it is very well executed. The seats are as yet unpainted, but I suppose they will not long remain so.

I slept at the Presbytery, W. Parsons having been kind enough to get a bed made up for me on a sofa in one of his rooms.

Saturday 19th

Rose at $7^{H}.30$. And not finding any washing materials in the room I went over to an hotel the opposite side of the street, where I got a room to make my toilet for the use of which I had to pay 1^{P}. Not having any razors with me, I asked one of the waiters within to lend me one, or if he could not to get a barber.

---

261. In the nineteenth century, 'lions' meant famous people, celebrities.
262. The bird Athy is referring to would likely have been either a Southern Boobook Owl or a Tawny Frogmouth. Both these birds could be described as having a 'moe poke' call.
263. This Church to which Athy refers is St Francis' Church at 326 Lonsdale Street Melbourne.

So after waiting a long time and neither razors nor barber coming I rang the bell again, when up came a more flourishing waiter; who apologised by saying that the other waiter was a German, that he did not understand me. So off he went and in two minutes brought me up a capital razor.

Just afterwards up came the barber, a nigger, a yankee, whose sign over the shop is 'I guess we can do it'. While he brought with him a bottle of stuff to wash my head with which by the way was a very pleasant operation, after which he shampooed my head, which consists in pressing it all over lightly with his fingers. As soon as he had finished I asked him what was to pay, and only think he demanded the enormous sum of 7^{P} for about a half hours work.

This next entry is made more than 9 months later, by which time Athy is living in Sydney. Although not recorded by Athy in this Diary, the Phoenix sailed from Port Phillip on 21 January and arrived in Sydney on 26 January 1856.

November

Tuesday 4

Monthly recreation day.

Having permission for an aquatic excursion to day, Father Sub prior, Brother Anselm and the Postulants started at about 9^{H}.30^{M} for Spectacle Island up what is called "the river", though in reality it is a narrow arm of the sea which runs up to Parramatta, we took our provisions with us as we determined to make a day of it.[264] Shortly after our arrival at the Island Father Sub Prior took another of the Postulants and myself to visit the establishment of the Marist Fathers, which is about three miles farther up the "river". Brother Anselm and the rest remained.

We arrived at the Monastery, or whatever it is called, just in time for dinner and right hospitably were we entertained by the fathers. There are but two there at present both Frenchmen indeed all the Marists of this mission are either French or Italian.

264. Spectacle Island is an island in Sydney Harbour. It lies in the main channel of the western section of the harbour, upstream of the Harbour Bridge. It lies in the lower reaches of the Parramatta River, as it enters the Harbour proper.

They are under the French Bishop Dr Battallin, a fine Patriarchal looking man with a long beard, I saw him here once when on a visit to the Archbishop, one of whose suffragans he is.[265]

The Marists have a nice secluded little spot here of about thirty acres. The house is prettily situated on a little hill at the head of a small inlet. They have made an avenue up to the house each side lined with orange trees. They have also a vineyard. The live quite an eremitical life here as they seldom are troubled with incursions of strangers being quite out of the world.

Their chapel is a very small unpretending little place detached from the house but quite close to it. We made our visit to the Blessed Sacrament after dinner when one of the Priests jabbered a lot of Prayers half latin half French, but I am blessed if I could make out the whole of them as I could only catch a latin word here and there.

After dinner we took our departure to rejoin our companions at the Spec's where we arrived about $2^{H}.0^{M}$.

We remained a little time on the Island, then set sail and reached St Mary's about 6^{H} just in time for Vespers.

I forgot to day that on leaving the house of the hospitable Marists we found our boat aground so the three of us had to take off our shoes & stockings and waded into the water to get her afloat again. Which feat we had likewise to perform when leaving Spectacle Island.

There are a good number of ships at present in the harbour two Frigates, The *Electra* of 86 guns and a smaller one the name of which I have not ascertained.

There are two Catholic officers on board the former one a W. Cholmely, who is I believe first-lieutenant. I suppose he is of the Cholmely's of Brandsby Yorkshire.

We also saw the *Sultana* the Australian Packet that left Liverpool about a week before we did last year.[266] She has been home and out

265. Athy is referring to Bishop Pierre Bataillon. See p 48 Athy Biography for more information.

266. The *Sultana* arrived in Sydney on 3 November 1856. The vessel made the run to Sydney regularly; it arrived on 26 May 1855, 4 July 1856 and again 3 November 1856. According to http://mariners.records.nsw.gov.au the vessel set out from London for each trip. Accessed 20 September 2015.

again. There also was an emigrant ship the *Winifred*, which appeared crowded with emigrants mostly english, they say.[267]

Brother John went to day to the farm at Subiaco, tenanted by his father, to recruit his health.[268]

267. This vessel arrived in Sydney on 3 November 1856.
268. Brother John was the grandson of Michael Dwyer (c1772 – 1825), the 'Wicklow Chief' who was sentenced to exile in Australia in 1806 for his part in the rebellion at Wicklow, Ireland in 1798 and the subsequent guerrilla fighting in the hills around Wicklow.
     Michael John Dwyer was born in Sydney in 1832, was educated at St Mary's and joined the Benedictines. He took the name of John in religion, was raised to the Deaconate in 1857 and ordained a Priest in 1859. He was later Dean of St Mary's Cathedral and died in 1884.
     http://adb.anu.edu.au/biography/dwyer-michael-12896 Accessed 31 May 2017
     St Mary's Cathedral Ordination Ceremony, Empire 30 June 1857 p 5.
     Death of Dean Dwyer OSB, The *Freeman's Journal* 19 April 1884 p 15.
     Life and Labours of the Late Dean Dwyer OSB, The *Freeman's Journal* 26 April 1884 p 15.

dinner time so I shall shut up for the present
4.30 Dinner - Mutton Roast - Boil. Corn Beef - Fowl
Bacon - Some Kin of Pie. Curry - Stew. The Archbishop
had something I can own I dont know what - before him
Potatoes Roast Cabbage - Turnips Carrots - Puddings - Sago
& Rice - ~~Tarts - Preserves and~~ Tarts, preserved plums
& cherry - Wines Port & Sherry - Beer & Porter
After dinner the breeze was very light - There
was a very pretty Sunset - As yet I have
seen none equal to the Sunsets of dear Auld Reekie
tropical though these are — 8.0 Rate 5 ½ Knots
7.30 Tea after Tea I went on deck smoked a
little and meditated somewhat on the approaching
delights of tomorrow - 8. 9. Rate - 6 ½ Knots
11. 9. Rest ———
~~6.30~~ So

Sources

Birt, Henry Norbert. *Benedictine Pioneers in Australia* (London: Herbert & Daniel, 1911).

Cash, Damien. *A Guide to St Francis' Church Melbourne, Australia* (Melbourne: Blessed Sacrament Congregation, 2012).

Cooke, Brian. *The Grand Crimean Central Railway: the story of the railway built by the British at Balaklava during the Crimean War of 1854-56* (Cheshire, UK: Cavalier House,1997).

Fletcher, John. *St James' Church Forest Lodge, A Chronicle 1877-1977.* (Sydney, 1977).

Gillow, Joseph. *A Literary and Biographical History, or Bibliographical Dictionary of the English Catholics from the Breach with Rome, in 1534 to the Present Time,* 4 volumes (London: Burns & Oates, 1885–1902). p 297 - 307 Volume 4. Accessed 30 November 2014 online at: <https://archive.org/search.php?query=A%20literary%20and%20biographical%20history%2c%20or%20bibliographical%20dictionary%2c%20of%20the%20English%20Catholics%20from%20the%20breach%20with%20Rome%20AND%20collection:toronto>

Hoban Mary. *Fifty One Pieces of Wedding Cake* (Kilmore, Vic: Lowden Publishing, 1973).

Hoctor Shane P. *Joyful, Sorrowful, Glorious. A History of the St Mary's Parish, Kyneton 1852–1977* (Kyneton: St Mary's Parish, 1977).

Hosie, John. *Challenge: The Marists in Colonial Australia* (Sydney: Allen & Unwin, 1987).

Marcil, Eileen Reid. *The Charley-Man: A History of Wooden Shipbuilding at Quebec 1763–1893* (Ontario: Quarry Press, 1995).

Moran, Patrick Francis. *History of the Catholic Church in Australasia* (Sydney: Oceanic Publishing, 1894).

O'Farrell, Patrick. *The Catholic Church in Australia, A Short History 1788–1967* (Melbourne: Nelson, 1968).

O'Sullivan, MD. *Old Galway, The History of a Norman Colony in Ireland.* Facsimile Edition (Cambridge: Heffer & Sons Ltd, 1942).

Schofield, Nicholas. *William Lockhart, First Fruits of the Oxford Movement* (Leominster, Herefordshire: Gracewing, 2011).

Shanahan, Mary. *Out of Time, Out of Place: Henry Gregory and the Benedictine Order in Colonial Australia* (Canberra: ANU Press, 1970).

Wiltgen, Ralph. *The Founding of the Roman Catholic Church in Oceania 1825 to 1850* (Canberra: ANU Press, 1979).

Wiltgen, Ralph. *The Founding of the Roman Catholic Church in Melanesia and Micronesia, 1850–1875* (Eugene, Oregon: Pickwick Publishing, 2007).

Wright, Esther Clark. *Saint John Ships and Their Builders* (Nova Scotia, Canada: Wolfville, 1976.

Wright, Esther Clark. *The Ships of St Martins, Ship Building and a List of Vessels Built at St Martins, New Brunswick, 1800-1899* (St John, Canada: New Brunswick Museum, 1976).

Editorial Committee, Sr Xavier Compton. *The Letters of John Bede Polding OSB*, Volumes 1, 2 and 3 (Sydney: Sisters of the Good Samaritan, Sydney 1994–1998).

Austral Light
Downside Review
Empire
Evening News
Freeman's Journal
Green Sash
Illawarra Mercury
Manly, Journal of St Patrick's Seminary
Sydney Morning Herald
Tjurunga
Webster's New International Dictionary, Second Edition 1934.
Wikipedia

Definitions in the Footnotes to the Journal without attribution are from *Webster's New International Dictionary*, Second Edition 1934.

Information and guidance on Liturgical matters was provided by Fr Colin Fowler OP.

Novr Wedns

[W]ednesday 19th Rose at 7-50 — M. Prayers. The
[q]uantity of water we have been receiving this
[w]eek past is very small indeed — Scarcely suffi-
[cien]t. On Deck All sails set wind N. E by N. Course S. W. b W
[Ra]te 7½ Knots Saw two Shoals of flying Fish Lady
[pre]tty looking things they are about the size of
[a] large Sardine — Bro Saw M E L. on deck —
[Bre]akfast. 8.30. Fare Mutton chops — Broiled Ham & Eggs
[Bo]iled Potatoes — Cold Tongue. Curry & Rice — Rice
[Bre]ad White and Black. Ship biscuit. Tea & c —
[Sa]w some kind of Petrels about the Ship. — 11. Studying
[on] Deck. 1. Study. 2. Read my Hours to the Archbishop
[an]d read 3 chaps of Eccles — 3-20. Went on Deck
[an]d found the Course of Vessel changed to S. & by W ½ W.
[1]2 Lat 17-48 — Long 22 & a few Miles — Saw lots
[of] flying fish to day they are very curious looking
things and very pretty — They fly very fast — They
[ar]e started by the Vessel just fly about 10 or 15
[ya]rds and then light in the water again Their
[w]ings are white something like gauze —

Appendix 1

Pecksniff

Seth Pecksniff was a major character in the English writer Charles Dickens', *The Life and Adventures of Martin Chuzzlewit*, published in serial form in 1843, then as a novel in 1844.

Dickens' Pecksniff

Dickens portrayed Pecksniff as a hypocritical, scheming person who feigned compassion and solicitous concern for others, but used these admirable qualities as a screen for gaining personal advantage at every possible opportunity. He presented himself as a morally sound, worthy, upright citizen, someone to be respected. A socially acceptable, indeed, he hoped an admired character that would be considered a pillar of the community.

Athy's Pecksniff

Athy uses the word 'Pecksniff' extensively in his Journal – the term is used over 60 times, being used as various parts of speech. For him to have used it so often, one must assume that the term was in common usage in the 1850's, at least amongst his family for whom the Journal was intended.

At the time of writing the Journal, Athy was considering a commitment to religious life as a Benedictine priest. During the voyage on the *Phoenix*, under the tutelage of Archbishop Polding, Athy was being schooled in Latin as well as studying texts that would have been intended to develop his spiritual life.

In using the term 'Pecksniff', I do not think that Athy was actually reading Dickens' work but rather intended to convey, with a touch of wry humour and perhaps irony, the suggestion of trying to develop attributes such as piety and humility, knowing his own imperfections. I think Athy was at heart an uncomplicated person. Athy was not suggesting that he, or others on the *Phoenix*, were hypocritical, but rather he saw the paradox of the real beside the ideal. I consider that he saw some of these disciplines as being at odds with his own flawed character, which he alluded to from time to time.

I interpret Athy's use of the word 'Pecksniff' to convey various shades of meaning. In some instances it seems he meant that he was reading material of a spiritual nature. At other times it indicated an examination of conscience, perhaps meditation, concentrating his mind on spiritual ideals. I do not consider Athy was inferring that he was developing pious thoughts and ideals but not actually intending to carry them through into his life, rather he was reading spiritual works, forming his mind on what God wanted of him, but was well aware of the gap between the ideal and the real. I think he was using a little self deprecating humour.

I consider his view was that an affect of piety and removal from the normal human enjoyments of life were an artifice and the Benedictines did not hold such views. Another subtle meaning attached to the word emerges in his use of it to describe activities at Christmas, a time of giving good wishes to those with whom he was travelling. He certainly did not see it as a negative concept.

Charles Dickens, *The Life and Adventures of Martin Chuzzlewit*. London 1951.

H M

4.30 – Dinner Tea Roast leg Mutton. Boiled Turkey – boiled Tea

Mustard. Veal – Bacon – Curry – Rice – Puddings

Rice & Sago or Tapioca – Tarts – Vegetables – Potatoes Turnips

and Carrots – Cabbage – Ale & Port – Wine – Port & Sherry –

No dessert – After Dinner went on deck – Mr

Gregory, who by the bye is the life and soul of

whole party – got up a lark which gave us

all ~~plent~~ plenty of exercise – He had an

india rubber ball, hollow, this he used

to fill with water, it had a very small hole

~~which~~ through which when squeezed, it

discharged the water in a jet and wet you

all – He went about the deck squirting this

at every one – There was much to running

about to get out of the way ———

H m

7.30 Tea – Bread & Biscuits – Sliced Tongue – Yarmouth Bl –

Portable – Port & Sherry – H m 11.30 To Bed

Rate of sailing about 7 knots

S.W.

45

Nov

Saturday 17 Arose at 7.0. Morning very fine breeze light from the E. 8. Bkfst. Chops – Liver & bacon cold tongue – Curry Rice &c – 10.0 Oh dear Oh this tropical weather is enough to kill me, here I am in my cabin writing this and perspiring like an ox. I have been so for the last three or four days when it will stop I do not know but I fancy that I shall be reduced in size considerably. In the last two nights I could not attempt to sleep in my berth so very hot has the weather become. I took my pillow and rug and lay myself to down on the couches in cabin the saloon and slept there with my head beneath the ventilator. I shall do the same so long as the hot weather continues – Reading Bible Bible 12 [illegible] [illegible] [illegible] No lessons today. Confessions [illegible] [illegible] lots of jottings have been [illegible] [illegible]

weather excessively hot ship badly making
any way I shall sleep tonight in the Cuddy I
cannot stand these small Cabins in such
very hot weather — I am writing this on Tuesday
20 Nov The weather was so hot that one
can scarcely do anything — I forgot the bottle
of Tonic

~~25~~ 3 Dec
Sunday continued
fearing that you may not decipher the two last words they are
"long winded" Sermon – I rather think it was one of
Archer's – 12.40. Lunch
Latitude 30-19 Long..
As I was coming down to breakfast, just as
I was entering the door of the house covering the
stairs the Ship gave a lurch that brought my
head in contact with the top of the door with
a violence that knocked me down – But I was
soon allright again – One of our mates a Mr
Murphy is laid up, infact he has been laid up for
some days. The ~~effects~~ combined effects I think
of having the fire engine played on his person
every morning, and playing at least the monkey
and such like juvenile sports unsuitable
I think to people of forty years – Besides on
time would do for these violent games
but immediately after dinner –
I have just taken about an hour's snooze
I really felt so overpowered that I was obliged,

Sundy continued Dec 11 84

in order to be fit for anything, to survive in way for a while - It is now 11.20. p.m. & I have just come down to turn in, but first I must write up the rest of to days journal Well to commence with dinner - Fam Soup which was very good - Roast - Porky, fresh, Boiled Mutton. Corn Beef - Pickled Pork - Goose Curry - Vegetables Carrotts & Potatoes - Sweets A kind of Plum-pudding - Tapiocca pudding Some kind of tarts - Cheese - Wine Port Sherry. Champagne - Ale - Porter - dessert Nuts - Almonds - Raisins - Figs - At 5-15 On deck lounging - there being a heavy sea on & the vessel pitching a good deal which she is doing likewise at this moment

7.10 Tea - Bread - Biscuits - Butter, salt, Marmalade

8.15 Pecksniff and Rosary till the ... -

9. Night prayers - Afterwards I went on deck till 11.20. And indulged in Pipe & Cigar - Now good night I am off to bed -

December

Christmas Day – 12th Midnight Mass – His Grace – Music – ~~Adeste fideles~~ "Venite exultemus Domino" – Adeste fideles – Laudate Dominum – It was a glorious thing to hear Mass and go to Communion at midnight, on the solitary ocean – Besides they say that we are in the same meridian as the part of the Holy Land in which Our Lord was born – There was a very good congregation for although it was kept as secret as possible yet ~~it was~~ somehow or other ~~got wind~~ the steerage and second cabin folks got wind of it and "Paddy" came crushing in – All of our party except the priests, each of whom ~~are~~ are to celebrate, went to Communion and likewise a large number of the Irish – ~~It was a~~ It is really a spiritual feast, and if it is possible to commit, a if there is such a sin, or spiritual gluttony I shall commit it – Father Melitus Corish will celebrate at 5.30 – Father Kickings at 6. Father McGuire at 6.30 Father Newman 7.0 Dr. Gregory 7.30 – which will be the last –

After Communion at Midnight, thanksgiving finished we ate a few cakes and then laid down, I only threw myself on my bed as I wished to be up in time for the Masses — 6-30 The Mass at 6-30 was given out on the eve, as the Mass at which any that wished could go to Communion — and a great number went — a few likewise went to Communion at 7-30 — It is the first time that I have been to Communion at Midnight since I left Sidon — I suppose that you have had all kinds of Pecksniffs and of the richest description in London, — and Midnight Mass too — It is so delightful to go to Communion about the very time that our Divine Redeemer came into the world — I do not suppose that any voyagers ever had half the opportunity that we have had of "making our souls — The sea rolled a little yet from fortunately not sufficiently to prevent the celebration of the sacred Mysteries

1856 January

Saturday 5th 7.45 Pecksniff. 8.30 breakfast. Tea. Pork Chops. Broiled Ham Hash, Curry, Red Herrings. Meat Cold. Tongue, Pork, Beef. There was a calm this morning till about 9.0 when a breeze sprung up carrying us at about 8 knots — which goes on to this moment. Course Compass E.S.E. that is Due E. Some Albatross and green(?) *Devils* following us in our wake. 12.0 Lunch. Afternoon Pecksniff. till 4.30. Dinner. Tea. Soup. Roast Pork. Pie. Broiled Fowl Hashed — Corn Beef — Pickled Pork. Pat.(?) Sherry etc — Cheese. After dinner heavy squalls came on which lasted the whole evening and night. ~~Long. 93~~ Longitude about 93. Lat 44½(?) — This horrible weather continues I fear that we shall not have Mass tomorrow

1850 January —

Sunday 6th In consequence of the rolling of the Ship we had not Mass to-day. Rose at 7-50. Pecksniff till 8-30. Breakfast. Fav Pork Chops - Broiled Ham, Hot Hash - Dry Hash - Sliced Corn beef & Pork. Cold Steamboat - Mashed Potatoes baked. After breakfast sauntered about till 11 o'clock when we had prayers for the Million and a long winded Sermon, I do not know the name of the author. Says the Adeste Fideles - Alma Redemptoris &c. There is a heavy breeze to-day causing a great swell at breakfast time every now and again we had to hold hard or some of the Dishes would have been swept clear off the table. It makes me laugh tremendously to see the grimaces the Captain makes during these lurches. He appears to be in the most intense agony, and in reality I

Thursday 17 - 3.10 Hour - Rose as I could not sleep in consequence of the noise and stamping of men over my head on deck. ~~the~~ I found that it was caused by a very violent breeze which had sprung up suddenly so much so as to make it necessary to come about and stand out to sea again - The wind from S. W. after we tacked the first we have made since we left the ~~Smalls~~ Smalls, islands or rocks at the mouth of the Bristol channel we stand S. W is now certain that we shall not get to Melbourne today; it appears ~~that~~ that there was some mistake in the middle watch as about 4.0 A.M. we passed the heads at Port Philip, being the entrance to Melbourne - I do not as yet know why we could not have entered with a S.W. Breeze. We have caught a good number of ~~Boncenta~~ today - It is a most queer looking fish

in Colour very much like a Hake the
head a good deal sharper than that of
the hake an the Tail like 
the large ones are about the size of a
small Hake — There are ~~now~~ no less
than six lines out astern, which are
always getting foul of each other
The Breeze still continues very heavy 5 a.m.
we have been obliged to take in
ever so much sail and likewise to
take in reefs — I assure you we were
were in no very pleasant position this
morning being at one time ~~[illegible]~~ rather
too close to an ugly looking reef
well we were obliged to stand out to sea again
as it blew so very hard, we were afraid to venture
on entering the harbour but about 3 P.M. the
weather moderated somewhat ~~but~~ — well
we have had some sport today catching
three Bonacouttas and we had some of

27. ×

under God I owe so much; without taking one look at him — he talked a good deal about Sledon, our old friends there and the retreat I went through there and which Mr ~~Pass~~ Parsons said was the one which brought me out here — his spirits seem completely gone — and no wonder — may those who so foully wronged him repent while there is yet time, a fearful will be their fate — Well ~~we~~ as soon as we had taken a mouthfull one of the priests escorted us through Melbourne to show us the lions; I must say ~~that for~~ the progress made by this city since first founded greatly astonished me — There are about One hundred and twenty thousand inhabitants — The streets are fine and wide; but this is no drawback the great quantity of dry sand on them and which with the least wind blows about and fairly blinds you — The exhibition building is also very fine - Built in the style of ~~ab~~ that class of buildings called Crystal palaces — I bought a cigar or two there really very good ones and cheap enough - Our Rev Cicerone took us to see the seminary, which promises to be a very fine building, it is not half finished In the garden he had a tame Kangaroo, a queer looking animal it is - And in his room an Australian bird called "More Pork" of the owl species. A mopeing bird - Well we afterwards walked about the Town till 4.30 when we went to the Presbytery to dine - The church is a ~~pret~~ pretty one the ceiling being being of ~~bor~~ Cedar - and nicely carved — It is got up in

20th 19 [illegible] Nov

Monday rose at 8.30. All sails set weather fair
Lat. Long - Breakfast as usual and the
same of the other meals — I say the
Drawing office now regularly with the
Archbishop & Benedictines — I forgot to
mention that for some time back when
much larger days feels light and at
½ 5. Am. Weather excessively hot - Every one
perspiring profusely

Tuesday 20 Rose at 7.0. Slept last night
on the form in the buddy - Meal as
usual - Nothing particular today We
expect to cross the Line tomorrow
I hear that the sailors will not be
permitted to play any tricks — Lighter in
long Homeward Bound —